You Can Never Go Back

'Sally Timmel has written a treasure trove of strategies and insights of how to campaign for social justice. The story of her life gives true meaning to what it means to be an activist with a commitment to social justice in times such as ours. It is fascinating that even though the strategies differ from the United States of America to Africa, they still focus on bridging the gap between people and policies, between economic and social groups, and between justice and oppression. Sally was indeed always the doer, planner to the last detail, organizer, results oriented and good with figures. The lessons learnt as described from each experience are the great pearls in the book that others can use in the unending struggle for justice. This book begs the question as to whether activism is a profession or a calling.

'Besides her nature as a meticulous planner and her penchant for details, the book lays bare the other side of Sally as a deeply caring and loving partner to Anne. Such transparency of emotional relationships in the life of a transformational leader is rare, particularly when these relationships challenge prevailing ways of being. Sally shows courage and reveals how her co-dependency with Anne changed through their separations into interdependence, like two strong but separate trees. Though unintentional, the book reveals how women network through long-lasting friendships to bring about the change they want to see in society. Sally's life is woven together through a network of women's organizations such as the Young Women's Christian Association, Church Women United and the Grail. Her deep appreciation for her friends and their roles in her life comes to the fore in the book.

'Sally Timmel is respected internationally by development practitioners for her work in transformational pedagogy through the volumes of *Training for Transformation* she authored with Anne Hope and the many workshops they ran to promote and instill critical consciousness in institutions and in their participants. Some of their approaches to critical analysis are well described in the book. I and many others are great beneficiaries of the expertise they crafted together with their co-learners. Our commitment to social justice and empowerment of the oppressed is founded in this tradition. The book enumerates the many initiatives she undertook that continue even today.'

'In this riveting account, Timmel traces the experiences and questions that drew her out from a small town in Wisconsin to places all over the globe. Through her journey we learn that the path to creating transformative social change is as much grit as it is one's formative values, as much perseverance and strategic thinking as it is partnerships, collaborations, and bringing communities together to address real needs. A delight to read.'

You Can Never Go Back

The autobiography of the co-founder of the Grail Conference and Retreat Centre, and Training for Transformation

Sally J. Timmel

DARTON · LONGMAN + TODD

First published in 2021 by
Darton, Longman and Todd Ltd
1 Spencer Court
140 – 142 Wandsworth High Street
London SW18 4JJ

ISBN: 978-1-913657-02-4

A catalogue record for this book is available from the British Library

Phototypeset by Kerrypress, St Albans
Printed and bound by Bell & Bain, Glasgow

Contents

Preface

More than a memoir, Sally Timmel brings a dispassionate eye to her life story as a creative, effective activist. She unrolls the blueprint of a mid-twentieth century US woman who grew beyond a parochial midwestern upbringing into a global citizen before most people knew such passports existed.

Her early insight into the different circumstances of those who are rich and poor, privileged and oppressed began a lifelong pursuit of empowerment and justice. Education at a women's college and work with the YWCA, later with Church Women United, provided Sally with a firm feminist intellectual and activist foundation even if the vocabulary for it came later. A stint in the Peace Corps in Ethiopia and subsequent travel in the Far East made her aware of the toxicity of colonialism and the power of solidarity.

It took falling in love with her longtime partner Anne Hope to nudge Sally in even broader, newer circles. Membership in the Grail, an international women's organization, provided Sally with additional platforms to actualize her many talents. She and Anne worked for years in Africa, especially Kenya and South Africa, to create Training for Transformation, a movement 'working for social justice through grassroots community education. Sally became what she terms a 'social inventor,' following her teenage dream of becoming an inventor, but of projects, organizations, and social change instead of things.

As an international couple, not to mention as two women, who were in disfavor in several countries because of their commitment to overcome apartheid and bring about free societies, they learned to be creative to thrive. Creative they were time after time, project after project, move after move, living simply but well.

Sally is a doer, someone who has never met a challenge she could not find five ways to meet. This gave her the ability to meld in ideas from her teammates and take in new information even though she did not take 'no' for an answer. Yet she is rigorously honest about her own limitations. In midlife, she realized she needed to attend to her own health, and find her own path independent of Anne. So she did, and when they resumed their common life several years later it was healthier and perhaps more productive than ever. Contrast that with so many clueless activists who are married to their work, the cause, at the expense of themselves and their loved ones.

Sally writes as if her biography were just another story of a woman of a certain vintage. But astute readers will realize that hers is a remarkable life, an example of how consciousness keeps expanding and justice keeps gnawing. She is like other wonderful women of my acquaintance, many religiously related whether nuns, Grail members, or Protestant church women, who had similar experiences. They travelled widely, developed deep and long-lasting commitments to people and to countries that others still cannot find on a map. Their contributions as workers, role models, and now as sages have shaped those of us who follow.

Thanks to Sally for laying out the contours of an activist vocation. Special thanks for embodying the words of Spanish Jesuit Superior General Pedro Arrupe:

What you are in love with,
what seizes your imagination,
will affect everything.
It will decide what will get you out of bed in the morning,
what you do with your evenings,
how you spend your weekend,
what you read, who you know,
what breaks your heart,
and what amazes you with joy and gratitude.

Fall in love,
stay in love,
and it will decide everything.

Sally fell in love with the world. She stayed in love with Anne Hope. And what a difference it all makes.

Mary E. Hunt, Ph.D.
Co-director, Women's Alliance for Theology, Ethics and Ritual
(WATER), Silver Spring, MD, USA

Pre-amble

I find this word, pre-amble, a fitting way to start. We humans amble through this world, and as we are but like a small grain of sand on a beach, and our earth, also like a small grain of sand emanating from the Big Bang into the Milky Way and then a planet growing life – into human life. As we 'amble', we make choices. For those of us not living at a survival level, these choices are often ethical. So, each day, week, year, or turning point will confront us with ethical choices. We miss them often, but sometimes in our lives, and sometimes, we choose a path that is on the side of the oppressed. And later, we can only say, we did our best.

As I write this autobiography, I am living at an intentional retirement community in southern California called Pilgrim Place. A tradition has been established for a resident most months to give a one-hour talk about their lives. I gave my talk in January 2020 and this helped me to ask myself: Where did I come from? Who are my people (or where do I belong)? Where am I going? These questions that arose in my mind have pricked my imagination. In July 2019, I had two heart attacks within 12 hours. A few weeks later, I had a Skype session with my psychotherapist who lived in Cape Town. She said that I had allowed my partner for 46 years, Anne Hope, to capture half my heart. Anne had died in December 2015. My therapist then said I needed to write my autobiography. That did it, and so this book was born.

A mystery

In 1972, I was sitting at a café on an island just off of Mozambique. I was with my partner, Anne Hope, who was South African. At that time, we had been partners for 3 years. As we finished eating, Anne leaned over our small table and whispered to me, 'Sally, don't look now, but behind you are two South African Special Branch detectives. Let's finish eating quickly and go down to the beach where we cannot be heard.'

We did just that and in our room that night spoke of trivia as we assumed our room was bugged. The next day as we crossed over to the mainland to our two cars, we hugged and went our separate ways: Anne to South Africa and me to Swaziland. Each of us watched with grins on our faces as the two detectives scratched their heads trying to figure out which of us to follow. A small laugh on our part, but of course, no victory. Unbeknownst to me, I would be given notice to be a prohibited immigrant in Swaziland upon return, and Anne had been served her notice earlier. Within a year, she had her South African citizenship revoked. But that is getting ahead of this story.

How did this small-town girl from the United States end up being tracked down by South African apartheid government police in Mozambique?

Grounding

What shapes or 'forms' a person is an intriguing question. As a 94-year-old wise woman commented frequently, it comes from your 'line' – who came before you. I didn't have what might be called a distinguished background. One set of grandparents came from Germany to the USA and settled in lower Wisconsin as farmers. My other grandfather ran a haberdashery in the same area. However, this second set of grandparents had a father who was an Italian peddler.

I have said for years, thank the Lord, I am not 100 per cent German. Well, no one is 100 anything. But in close proximity – being only 'German' would be hard to live with: super-efficient, super direct and very willing to give commands. Ah, but I feel blessed with this wing from an Italian who I imagine had a flair, used his arms and hands to speak, and always with a sense of humor to lighten those commands from that German strand. Though, sadly, that didn't always work. And this great-grandfather also was a peddler. Now, isn't that what a cheerleader is? Or someone who organizes on the side of the poor? Or demands participatory processes to ensure the voices of the disenfranchised? My great-grandfather must have done pretty well, as this strand left me with enough gifts to help build some wonderful movements that affected different parts of the world.

And my other grandfather, Timmel, who was German, owned a farm outside Oconomowoc. With his nine children, he operated this farm until his oldest son decided he would be a farmer as well. So, my grandfather became a carpenter, which skills I assume he learned while building his own farmhouse and barns. Grandfather Timmel then built himself a house in Oconomowoc and helped my father build our family home as well. This strand gave me a huge interest in building throughout my life.

My father, Leo Timmel, grew up on this farm just outside of Oconomowoc, Wisconsin. Oconomowoc is a small, all-white town settled by Norwegians and Germans. The area was first inhabited by the Potowatomi and Winnebago Native Americans. There are three lakes that connect in this town and so the name, meant 'where the waters meet'. Later, when white settlers came, they made it a recreation area for people from Chicago and Milwaukee. My dad had six brothers and two sisters. Two of his brothers became Wisconsin Synod Lutheran ministers but somehow, my dad maintained friendships with people in the rival Evangelical Lutheran Church, so I was spared the rigid orthodoxy of the Wisconsin Synod sect. Most of his other brothers went to college in the 1920s and his two sisters became nurses.

Unlike his siblings, dad did not go to college. Because he had 'weak lungs', his parents sent him to Montana to an uncle's 20,000-acre ranch to become a cowboy, believing that the strenuous work would strengthen his lungs. He told us stories of riding out into the ranch for days, rustling cattle, sleeping under the stars, playing guitar, and singing songs in his good tenor voice. When he returned to Oconomowoc, he continued working on his father's farm. With his good sense of humor and enjoyment of interacting with people, he decided to become a barber in Oconomowoc. With only fourth-grade education and a cordial, gentle manner, he would thrive in that trade. In high school, I sometimes would feel ashamed that my father had 'low social status'. This changed immensely as I grew older.

In town, he had a good friend named Herb Otto. Herb married a woman who came from a family of six girls and one boy and introduced my dad to one of the sisters, Stella Sette. Stella had studied secretarial skills and had become the executive secretary to the president of the Heil furnace company in Milwaukee, thirty miles from Oconomowoc. The chemistry was there! They told of their courtship – ice-sailing on lakes, going golfing, and playing cards with friends. They married in 1934. My parents had very different temperaments and great affection for each other. Theirs was a loving home. With my grandfather's help, they built a family home six houses away from grandfather's house. They had their first child, Don, in 1937. They wanted to have a girl, and I came along in 1940.

My mother came from a family of six girls and one boy. Much later in her life, when I was in my thirties, my mom asked me repeatedly, 'Was I a good mother?' I would of course say, 'Sure', although she was the disciplinarian in our home. Then she would say, 'Well, ten months after I was born, my mother had twins. They were very, very small and were kept in shoe boxes in a dresser drawer in order to keep them alive. It was 1907. So, I had very little nurturing. I don't think I knew how to nurture.' I found this on the one hand quite insightful of my mother, and on the other hand, quite sad. This would also be an area I would question about my own life, liking to work with people in large groups but not being very good at mentoring people one-on-one.

Like most middle-class American women in the 1940s and 1950s, my mother left her job and became a full-time housewife. My father was now a full-time barber, but because his customers had more time on a Saturday to get a haircut, he took Thursday afternoons off. We kids loved those Thursday afternoons.

Throughout my years in my family home, I had my father's unconditional love. He had my back in difficult moments and nurturing tenderness always. My mother was focused on the tasks at hand, was disciplined and focused. I would hope to have both my father and mother in my 'character' but I think my mother's won out.

The early years that become a foundation

World War II was raging in Europe from 1939, the year before my birth, through August 1945. My family was mostly German and Germans were an enemy. Although both my parents and grandparents spoke German, they stopped speaking German during the war except when they had 'secrets' from my brother and me and they spoke in German. This, of course, increased our curiosity and helped us both to at least 'hear' German. Little did I know that German POWs were held in the Midwest and transferred to prison camps by train, sitting in the 'white' cars while black soldiers were consigned to the baggage car.

I was told quite often that my father's two sisters actually delivered me into this world. My father's two sisters who had become nurses, worked at Summit Hospital on Oconomowoc lake. The doctor was named Dr Love. Story has it, Dr Love stepped out of the room about the time I was ready to come into this world, and my aunts delivered me. I have in my imagination that they smiled with great delight and welcomed me. Being born must be very painful and going through that birth canal, no easy feat. To be greeted with such enthusiasm and praise, and feeling 'safe' probably gave this baby girl – me - a load of self-confidence. As I now reflect on this sense of feeling 'safe', I actually do not recall, ever, feeling afraid. I believe that my birth experience has given me a lot of self-confidence throughout my life.

I grew up in this idyllic small white, homogeneous town in Wisconsin with a population of then 3,000 people. The only 'big' differences were we were Lutherans (with 4 Lutheran churches) and the 'others' (one Catholic Church that I heard called 'damn-Catholics' -that was one word), and the other protestant churches (Methodist, Congregationalists, and Presbyterians housed in one church). In grade school, we walked to school, played on the playground, and learned arithmetic with flashcards. Our after-school activities were to play baseball in the park across the street from my house, hide-and-seek in the woods behind my house, or have picnics in the woods Saturday noon and family picnics in the park. As our street was near the end of the city, we played baseball in the streets as well.

In winter, my grade school friend, Susan, and I would ice skate to middle school. In looking back at this adventure, it probably took as long to skate across the lake as to walk around it. We had to sit in a snow bank, take off our boots, put on our skates, ice skate across the lake, and again, sit in a snow bank, take off our skates and put on our boots. All in freezing weather. Then as we skated across the lake, as the ice expanded as it froze more, we would hear big booms. We could see alarming new cracks suddenly in the ice appear before us. Rather tricky going. But this was growing up. Also in winter, we would go tobogganing down the hills of the golf courses or other parks in the area. Seeing those 'hills' as an adult, they really were small, but they were thrilling as a child. One's perspective of realities changes as we grew older. I recall that the snowbanks from shoveling the sidewalks seemed enormously high, way over my head, although I was probably only three or four feet tall then.

The park across the street was on a small hill that went down to a river. This river was originally narrow and somewhat shallow. Later when mail was carried by boat on this river, the river had been cut deeper to carry the mailboats. So this river was somewhat dangerous. I was not allowed to go down the hill to the river unless I was with an adult, in case I were to fall in. If I saw my grandfather fishing by the big tree, I sometimes joined him, though not for long, as fishing was quite tedious. Each summer, a group of Redemptorist priests would canoe down the river and come up the hill to play games with us kids. One time, my closest friend and I walked down to the river with the priests to say goodbye, and as we walked up the hill, there stood our mothers saying we had broken the rule by going down at the river without an adult. We tried to point that we had been with priests, but they had just paddled beyond what one could see. I was then given a spanking by my mother, the first and only one I remember. Being accused falsely can stick with one for a long time.

My brother and I were quite different, even in our early days. My mother was the parent who disciplined us. Sometimes my brother would do something that my mother thought was not right, so she would send him into the hall closet as a 'punishment'. I would then go around the house saying: 'I'm a good girl, mommy.' As my brother was four years older than me and much bigger physically, I would sometimes stay away from him, so I would not be teased or feel in a minor way, threatened. I think I grew up learning to either walk away if I saw conflict or cover myself that at least I was on the right side of 'the angels'. In hindsight, I am not sure if many of us learned how to deal with conflict, or even differences of opinion or styles of behavior.

Entering high school meant I had 'grown up'. I was determined to get better grades than my brother and get into the honor society. I studied hard and did both. At the same time, I sure wanted to be popular. I had been a cheerleader in middle school, but a cheerleader in high school was a very big deal for a 'girl'. With a loud voice and great enthusiasm, I went onto the high school stage, to be voted on (with 10+ other girls) by the whole school of 1,000 students. Well, I won, but I think mainly because of my booming voice, not my dexterity. A wee competitive streak seems to be always within me.

Cheerleaders followed all the football and basketball games at home and away. We kept our spirits up and always with optimism that our team would win. Later I have wondered whether this perseverance helped me to become a good fundraiser. Here your team has lost 9 games and you only have one last game to play for the season. There is one minute left to play in this last game and you are losing big time. But we still cheered as if this would make all the difference. That sense of purpose – perseverance – kept me going throughout my life.

During the summers before I turned 16 years old when I could get a summer job, there was sailing and water skiing with friends who lived on the lake and had boats. Idyllic though it was, I often did not go with the 'gang' to just swim. I actually found I enjoyed reading in the backyard and found it more fulfilling.

While in school, there were numerous dances. One time a group of us left a dance and went out to an apple orchard to 'steal a few apples'. This happened around midnight. Some other folks had been there before us, and the owner had called the police. The police arrived while we were stealing the apples. He took us to the house of the owner, who was a member of my church. Then the police took us to the police station. A policeman took my fingerprints and said after I told him my name, 'Oh, I get my haircut from your father'. Well, keeping this incident from my parents was going to be impossible. Then, the alarm at the bank went off, and the vice-president of that bank, my uncle, came into the police station at 2 o'clock in the morning and saw me. Living in a small town has lots of positive elements – support, friendly, and caring people. The downside, is everyone, but *everyone*, knows your business – knows about your life.

Many of my classmates got jobs over the summertime. Also, my parents insisted that I paid half of my college expenses so I needed a job to save enough to go to college. By law, one could not have a paying job until one was 16 years old. Fortunately, Oconomowoc had a recreation department that hired high school and older students to run morning recreational activities for younger kids. I got one of those jobs and especially liked the 12-14 year-olds. You could argue with them and try to talk them into being less counter dependent (takes one to know one).

I also taught tennis three afternoons a week and was a waitress in the evenings. One day, I went into the recreation director's office and he was slamming down his phone. I said, 'Bill, what's the matter?' He replied, 'My golf teacher just quit.' I responded, 'Oh, I will teach golf' (although I had never played before). He turned to me and said, 'You're on!' When I made it clear I had never played golf he stated, 'I will pay for you to have golf lessons at the private golf course. You just have to keep two lessons ahead of what you teach!' I did just that. What a gift! I hardly played in college, and of course, never in my 32 years in different African countries, but today, in retirement, I play and I enjoy it most of the time. The fundamentals are still there, like riding a bicycle.

In high school, I also developed a special friendship with a Catholic girl. I didn't know what this meant but I wanted to be with her most of the time. This 'being in love' during an era of strong heterosexual norms, was difficult to navigate. So having a 'boyfriend' was essential to keep to the outside world norms. I don't think it was internalized 'homophobia', but keeping up a front while living in two worlds. This may in part explain my next choice.

With my good grades, being a cheerleader, and belonging to a number of high school clubs, I got a partial scholarship to go to college. I applied to two colleges and was accepted by both. One was St Olaf College (a Lutheran College) where my brother attended and numerous friends planned to attend. The other was MacMurray (a Methodist Women's College) where one of my cousins, who was an idol of mine, had attended earlier. But I was torn. In early June, my father sat me down and said, 'Sally, you have to decide. I am going to flip a coin, and that will be the decision.' I gulped. I called out St Olaf as heads on the coin. He flipped the coin. It ended up heads for St Olaf - and at that moment, I blurted out, 'No, MacMurray'. Quite a brilliant way to force a choice by relying on listening to one's gut.

Broadening consciousness in one's formative years

When I was about 8 years old, my childhood best friend (who lived 2 houses from me in the woods) and I were walking to primary school. Three houses from my grandparents' house, I stopped. I looked at the grass and it appeared greener than ever before. And the sky looked a deeper blue. I marveled at this wonder. I stood still. Then we proceeded to walk to school. Those images of that verdant green grass and electric blue sky never left me. It was an early moment of seeing this world beyond just my Self.

My father bought 6 acres of fertile land one mile out of Oconomowoc. He and my mother farmed strawberries, raspberries and asparagus. He 'gave' me some land about 20 yards long by 3 yards wide to grow sweetcorn. I was 9 years old. He tilled that plot, and then I was to plant, weed, water (from hoses from our well that he had hand-dug to 30 feet). Then I picked the corn, carried my harvest on my bicycle in bags and one front basket into our neighborhood and sold the corn at 29 cents a dozen. I also had to put my earnings into US Savings Bonds that would mature in 10 years. From age 9-15, I planted, maintained, harvested and sold corn.

When I returned from the Peace Corps in Ethiopia in 1964, ten years later, I cashed in my 'corn money', that amounted to $250 (in 2020 worth about $2070). This was in 1965. This work taught me to be self-reliant and see a project through from its beginning to the very end. When cashing in those bonds, I realized that 'money' was not the object – indeed, it was almost irrelevant. The work ethic and learning skills in planning and use of time were burnt into my consciousness at a very early age by my 'corn' work. Of course, my parents lived through the Great Depression, which probably strengthened their determination that I learn those skills.

When we got television – I was about twelve – I watched a dramatization of Hans Christian Andersen's *The Little Match Girl*. This story captivated me. I deeply identified with this little match girl in the freezing cold with snow piling up everywhere, selling matches to get money to buy food for her family. I felt happy to be her. I imagined she was in Germany and identified with her commitment to helping others. Her bravery filled me with the belief that I too could make a difference to some people. Of course, the actual story is much sadder than this, but I blocked out its tragic ending and held the image of this heroic girl behaving as I wanted to behave.

My small town had two movie theaters. In the winter, one of them showed educational films for the kids on Saturday afternoon. I was probably about 14 years old. An important film for me was the life of Thomas Edison. The film showed how when Edison was a teenager, his mother had an attack of appendicitis during the night. They called the doctor who quickly put his mother on the dining room table and asked for all of the candles in the house be put in front of mirrors around the room that then reflected the candlelight back and forth. The film zoomed in on Thomas Edison's face, to show his mind trying to figure out 'light'. As my friend Susan and I walked home, I said to myself, I am going to become an inventor. I immediately went down to my father's wood bench in the basement. I grabbed some wood and hinges and a saw. I was going to invent an automatic page turner. So, I went to work that Saturday afternoon, and Sunday and a few days after school. By Thursday I had it completed, only to find it took three movements of my hands on my page turner to turn a page. Whoops. That didn't work. I remember putting all of my 'invention' in the waste barrel. Failure was not the word I used. In science, you have a hypothesis, try it out and move onto something else when it does not work. A great lesson that does not stop an inventor. It would not stop me, in different ways.

Then there was the television production of *Amahl and the Night Visitors*. This short opera tells the story of the three kings following a star to pay homage to a newborn child (Jesus). They stop at this widow's hut and ask to stay for the night. The widow has a child who has a bad leg and uses a crutch, but who is bright and curious. As the kings slept that night, the mother, as she sees all of the kings' gold, sings a lament asking if rich people know what to do with their gold. She continues by asking how that gold could feed a child or keep a home warm. Her dilemma is whether to try to take some of that gold, for her child.

I felt the widow's pathos, which had me question throughout my life, whom do I serve? What is the meaning of life? Is our vocation to be in solidarity with those at the bottom?

My parents were very regular churchgoers in a Lutheran church in our small town. We kids went to weekly youth programs, sang in choirs, and went to summer youth church camps. While at one of these camps, we were given a biblical verse and asked to go to a quiet spot outside and think about that passage. The verse I was given was: 'I was hungry, and you gave me food.' Quietly, on that small hillside, sitting in the warm rays of the sun, I said to myself, 'I am going to be a missionary, and work in Africa someday.' Later in this book, we will see how the 'missionary' part fell away.

Although this was almost a 'Lutheran' town, our neighbors were Catholic. Their daughter was thinking of becoming a nun. A number of nuns also visited them. I met them and thought them exotic and somehow their commitment to a different perspective of this world came across to me. I do not think I thought about this much, but their presence broke some stereotypes I had learned even at a young age and a small niggling feeling I had that there are many different ways to be.

We know early childhood often forms the values and character for the future adult. My mother always said to me, I was for the 'underdog'. Learning that the world was bigger than me, that feeling I was from a lineage of poor folks, and that I was 'called' to those who were disenfranchised became an underpinning of my life in the future. I also had learned the value of perseverance and was blessed with curiosity and an inventive mind. It was to be an effective combination.

Opening the mind

MacMurray College is in middle Illinois, near Springfield. MacMurray had just become a 'co-ordinate' college, which meant it admitted male students whose dorms were a bit far from the main campus and the women's campus. We shared the same faculty and classes but had separate dining rooms, newspapers, yearbooks, governance, and sports. Most of us women mainly kept to ourselves except when it came time to go to a dance.

Freshmen women were housed in an old building with high ceilings and common bathrooms. Joining clubs, participating in sports and choir were part of integrating into this new culture. There also was a small wing in the freshman dorm called the 'smoker' (and you can imagine what happened there). However, hot bridge games also occurred so it was a great place to get away from the books! There were four African-American freshmen students, who I got to know; however, having grown up in an all-white small town, I did not at that moment understand the Civil Rights Movement that was emerging. This was 1958, two years after Dr Martin Luther King Jr.'s Montgomery Bus Boycott. I sure was lagging behind. I was more taken aback by being 'Lutheran' in this Methodist school where both religion classes and compulsory weekly chapel were shaking my literal understanding of the Bible. A small clique of Lutherans would meet to discern our faith. Slowly, my understanding of my values and theology became more flexible. This started the shift in terms of openness to 'what is truth' and questioning my values.

I became very active in our student YWCA. I was moving towards acting on those values - my faith. I soon became an office bearer of the Y and was then elected its president by the entire student body. This afforded me the chance to attend regional and national meetings of the student Y. The YW, with the YMCA, was immersed in the Civil Rights movement in the US, along with the parallel anti-apartheid movement in South Africa. This brought not only a shift in awareness, but also deeper relationships with people of color and a huge jump into understanding 'who is your neighbor'.

After our freshman year, students were allowed to pick their own roommates and move into one of the other three dorms. These dorms were built with suites, that is, two bedrooms with an adjoining bathroom. It was always a priority to try to get a corner suite to have more windows. Somehow, my new roommate and two suitemates were able to get corner rooms. Being a Methodist College, there was no drinking and also no drinking within 24 hours of returning to campus from vacations. Having got into the 'habit' of beer drinking in high school, this was good for my head and soul.

My second year, I took a wide range of classes including one on the great books (like Socrates, Tolstoy, Flaubert, Thomas Hardy), chemistry, sociology and others. One day I was walking quickly to an Education Philosophy course, and I linked some insights from one of those great books, sociology and chemistry together. I have no recollection about what that insight was – but I felt I had made a big discovery. Wow! This ability to link disparate things together was something that stuck and felt powerful and important.

In my third year, I heard through my church about a workcamp to renovate an ancient church in Iceland. I applied and was accepted. I had to raise half of the amount of the cost, perhaps $1,000. I asked two aunts who had no children to donate some money to me, with one giving me a very small amount. Although disappointed, this first experience of fund raising taught me a lesson that you can ask for anything, if you can graciously accept a 'no'.

In Iceland, we were equal numbers of Icelanders, students from the United Kingdom and my group from the USA. We dug ditches in the early morning, had Bible studies, did more physical work, and had excursions around Iceland. We went to spas, walked in mountains and never saw the sunset as this was during the summer. To see the sun roaming around the edges of the horizon day and night was spectacular. Our sleeping rooms had velvet curtains, so sleep was possible. One evening while washing up the dishes with an Icelander on whom I had a crush, he said that Icelanders were very against the American presence in Iceland with our army base. I was very taken aback! I had no idea of global politics. 'Weren't we Americans wonderfully generous people?' I thought. I was hurt, and also shaken by his strong emotions about our presence. My distress and desire to understand why Icelanders saw my country differently stayed with me and became a prelude to further insights.

With this shaken perception of who I was as an 'American', and the new discovery of my faith and my religion at a Methodist college, I still was considering becoming a missionary after I left college. I recall that in my last year there were two classmates who planned to become Lutheran missionaries. They were quite pious and I did not feel much affinity with them. This was 1961-2. At this time, the Peace Corps was being established. Although I was not a big fan of John F. Kennedy (coming as I did from a Republican family), there was something about this big vision and openness to other cultures that struck my imagination. No one else at MacMurray was considering joining the Peace Corps. So, why not I?

I sent in my application and I indicated a few countries I was interested in serving. When my acceptance came through, I was placed in Ethiopia. Though I only had a vague thought of where that was, I looked it up on a map, and embraced this for my immediate future.

Becoming a global citizen

Our Peace Corps training was at George Washington University in Washington D.C. for two and half months in the summer of 1962. This was rigorous, with morning physical fitness classes on the college track held punctually at 6 a.m. Then after quick showers and breakfast, classes were conducted all day with study materials as well. There were 350 of us in this training, with an expected fallout rate of around 10 per cent.

We were fortunate to have Margaret Mead as one of our lecturers. I remember two main insights I gleaned from Dr Mead. She said we all have experienced cross-cultural shock through our parents. For example, one parent pushed toothpaste from the bottom up and neatly rolled the tube, and the other parent just squeezed from the middle, leaving somewhat of a mess. As a child, you had to decide whom you would emulate. She also shared that the first thing that might hit us upon arriving in a new culture would be the smell. She was absolutely correct. When we landed in Addis Ababa a few months later, the smell of eucalyptus burning permeated everywhere. It is a wonderful smell I still appreciate.

Our language classes were for Amharic, the language of Haile Selassie Emperor of Ethiopia. A very tough learning experience as the script and sounds were so different from English. The sounds had 'explosives' which took some manipulation of the tongue, cheeks, lips, and breath. Though learning the rudiments of Amharic didn't help the majority of us who were stationed in provinces that had different home languages. Later when the initial nine of us were stationed in Makelle, the capital of Tigre Province where the language of the area was Tigrean, we were not only at a loss linguistically, but in many ways, were perceived as an imposition from the ruling class. This conflict between different ethnic groups continues to this day between Tigreans and the national government.

As our group was one of the first to be sent to countries after pilot programs had been successful, President John F. Kennedy wished us well at a gathering in the White House South Rose Garden. I, of course, stretched out my hand for a brief shake. Most of us then boarded a Pan Am flight to Addis Ababa with a stopover in Athens. It was certainly a treat to explore the ruins and enjoy some Greek food. When we landed in Addis, we actually doubled the secondary school teaching force. Without any conscious intention from us as volunteers, this was a cultural invasion.

Ethiopia

In Addis, we continued to have language and other classes, went sightseeing, and had talks from Ethiopians as we acclimatized to our new country and the altitude. Within two weeks, we had been assigned to towns and cities throughout Ethiopia and put on buses to our destinations. In hindsight, I think the Peace Corps staff arranged these teams by stationing those who came from bigger or better-known universities in the larger cities, while at the same time paying attention to gender balance, subject matter and racial diversity.

The nine of us slated for Makelle, Tigre Province travelled to our destinations with other teams. Ethiopia is a very mountainous country. It had been colonized by the Italians for seven years. We marveled later that the Italians were not very 'good colonizers' as they did not lay down an administration or institutions to control the people. Instead they built fantastic roads through these mountains, started to build a few towns and left spaghetti restaurants scattered everywhere.

At this time, the division of wealth was still through a feudal system, with the Emperor owning more than half the land and farmers paying him for their use of it. The Coptic Christian Church owned the remaining land.

In the two-day bus ride to Makelle, we went through mountainous terrain with small villages en route. Every one of these towns had small shops and all had Coca-Cola signs. After seeing so many of these, it made one wonder if the USA was mainly exporting our 'vulgarities'. I recall being jarred by the presence of this American cultural and commercial icon.

We arrived in Makelle and were welcomed by local officials and some students. Initially we were housed in a basic local hotel, which had small rooms set around a small courtyard, and two common toilets. In a few days, a house was ready for us six women. We settled in and tried to figure out how to cook meals on a kerosene burner. After some furniture was installed, we realized we were quite a 'tourist' attraction for local children. We were to start teaching, but the school only had room for 1,000 students at a time and we needed space for both elementary and secondary students. The elementary students used the schoolrooms in the mornings and high school was held from 1-6 p.m. We met the doctors from Poland who staffed the one hospital in Makelle and two of us offered to help in the laboratory in the mornings. This proved to be a challenge, as there was very little equipment in the lab. We had to improvise, but almost every day for more than a year we helped as much as we could. Over time, we secured donations from other United States agencies to get more equipment to this hospital.

Once classes started, each afternoon began with an assembly where all the students were lined up in straight rows, a prayer given, and then systematically, each row marched into a classroom. I was to teach science to six classes with 40 students in each class. The classrooms held around 15 benches and small desks, meaning some benches held 3 students. Students were used to learning by rote. Teachers would write all their notes on the blackboard and students would copy those notes and memorize them for the final, and only, exam each year. Obviously, this was not the way we Americans were accustomed to learning. Our experience was giving frequent tests, students studying from books and asking questions to clarify what they had learned.

As I was a science teacher, I realized there were two things that made this in some ways easier, as well as in some ways more difficult. Giving homework and grading papers was much better for me than for my two roommates. They taught English and had to grade essays. For me, it was short answers: either a tibia is a bone in the lower leg or it is not. I thought using a laboratory was a very significant way to learn. I had been a lab technician in college, and although it was sometimes tedious, I integrated textbook information with factual insights under a microscope. However, the problem was having enough equipment. With another science teacher, we made a plan to find some hospitals in the larger city of Asmara that might have some microscopes, test tubes, kerosene burners, and the like. We asked the Peace Corps offices for assistance.

After many months, we had the rudimentary equipment to conduct lab classes in a room that had apparently been built as a lab, with 16 sinks, but of course it had no running water. With 40 students in each of my six science classes, I had to divide each class in half, or 12 lab classes a week. A slight overload. I learnt very quickly that teaching the same material 12 times was not just tedious, but very boring. I also became impatient with the later classes and couldn't understand why they might not understand something I had just explained 10 times, forgetting they were a different group of students. I quickly asked two students from the earlier classes to be co-teachers in the next classes. This got me off the hook, and was a great way for some students to internalize what they had learnt in the earlier classes.

But science was not the only class that missed equipment. This was a provincial school, which meant it did not have much infrastructure such as a library, enough desks, books for each student, or typewriters for commercial classes. We learned a great lesson about USAID. We worked with the Peace Corps representatives to Ethiopia and requested 40 typewriters for the Makelle school, as each class had 40 students. It took one year for 20 typewriters, 20 swivel chairs and 20 metal typewriting tables to arrive at our school. When we complained that we did not need the tables and chairs, but were told the corporation USAID purchased the typewriters from only sold them with the tables and chairs. Tables and chairs could have been made in our school shop, but we learned how USAID worked and how US dollars actually remained in the USA for corporations, but not for building up a local economy.

In my journal for October 1962 I wrote:

'And tonight I thank God for peace – for life – and happiness; for this is happiness. I thank God for a willing heart, a full stomach, a useful mind, and strong body. Why me in this world so full of struggles? To hear the wind blowing through the shutters as if it tells us of the forces of the world, to hear the howling hyenas wanting to fill their bellies, to feel the warmth of a candle as I read and the briskness of the air – the contrast of love and death, to see the whiteness of the moon over the sleeping town. I know why I live.

'It is humanity that howls out, it is the warmth of the light that answers in thought, and it is the challenge of the wind to control – for man was made to gain control of himself – to free himself of himself. Can the woman with the yoke of hemp ever be free of ignorance? She walks to the creek each morning (and I pass her to go study microbes through the microscope at the hospital) to answer the cries of her child. Can the student who starves for books and a full stomach ever learn the treasurers he tastes? But we try. We teach till we get hoarse and ache. We give only to gain an understanding that can never be replaced. This evening we sang as we did the dishes to keep all spirits raised ... to sleep with a wind encircling dreams of past and future and the present ... only to go forward.'

The big lesson

Three months into our arrival, a conflict was brewing. Some of the staff, including many of us Peace Corps volunteers, were concerned that the pass mark for moving to the next level, was set at 50 per cent. The teaching staff now was made up of nine of us from the USA (all Peace Corps volunteers), three Ethiopians, two Indians, and two others from Europe. Our headmaster, Ato Asfew, who was from the Amharic clan, was not clear whether the pass mark should stay at 50 per cent or be raised to 60 per cent. Staff meetings became heated, and more students started to rebel. We were shunned by some students, and insults were occasionally shouted at some of the volunteers.

Our headmaster didn't want to take a position and so the student anger started to be focused on him. The students went on strike, and the school was closed. Provincial and education officials came to the school to resolve the conflict. There was a tentative option for us as volunteers go to the northern city of Asmara in Eritrea until the dispute was settled. In January, our headmaster, Ato Asfew, was transferred to a different school. The pass mark stayed at 50 per cent.

At this stage, at a meeting of volunteers, Wendell Brooks, a black-American and a history teacher, suggested we needed to remember that we were guests in this country; since we were the majority on the teaching staff, we should not vote on any decisions. We could have our voice, but not vote. After some time, this became our practice. I have remembered that lesson. We needed to be aware that we brought a cultural invasion to Ethiopia, and without conscious intention, an extension of white Western power.

We continued

Kilimanjaro

In Makelle, we resumed teaching, holding laboratory classes, grading papers, having parties and going out on excursions and feeling we were getting on. Some Peace Corps volunteers from other places got cheap tickets to fly to Kenya for our upcoming one-month holiday. I signed up and found a friend to go with me. With five others, we also booked to climb Mount Kilimanjaro. My friend and I then hitchhiked to Uganda, toured a game park and the western area of the country.

Upon returning to Nairobi, we hopped on a bus that took us down to Moshi, Tanzania. There we geared up for our 5-day hike up Mount Kilimanjaro. The first day was through rainforests and then terrain like a moonscape. We had 3 or 4 guides who carried bedding and food supplies and cooked our meals. It was a real treat. The second day consisted of hours walking through the moonscape with a smaller mountain to our right and Kilimanjaro straight ahead. The third day we climbed to the third hut which was right on the mountainside. Our guides woke us the next morning at about 3 a.m. We began our ascent, and soon found we had to walk in a zigzag through the scree so as not to slip back. We were also at about 17,000 feet above sea level.

One of my fellow Peace Corps volunteers would put out his hand and tug me along. There were a few minutes where I do not remember even walking as the altitude started to affect me. We had stopped in a small cave for some very sugary tea, which helped. After a long struggle, we were on the top of the world – well – top of Kilimanjaro. We pulled out our cameras, took pictures of ourselves near a flag, and walked on the edge of the crater for a short time. Our guides then moved us along to hike down the scree and past our last hut down to the second hut. The final day we walked down to base camp, past that first hut we had stayed in. My ankles were now swollen like I had elephantitis. But what a spectacular experience.

Two of us then flew to Zanzibar, where 6 other volunteers had rented a former slave cottage on the ocean. We joined them on this lovely beach. The cottage was one long hall and a large, long veranda. We took out our sleeping bags and found spaces to sleep. Our daily breakfasts, lunches and suppers for 6 days were lobsters, baguettes, and coffee. I still have never tired of lobster.

Back to work

Arriving back in Makelle, we all gathered to share our holiday experiences. Then we were back to work with the same number of classes, 12 lab classes, and reduced work at the hospital lab. By this time, the first two Peace Corps doctors, Ron and Phil, had been able to secure several new staff at the hospital including an Ethiopian lab technician, and several Peace Corps nurses. They added to our weekend parties and dinner engagements.

On the morning of 22 November 1963, those of us in our house were having a late breakfast when Dr Ron rushed in and announced that President Kennedy had been shot in Dallas, Texas. We couldn't believe it. We immediately turned on the radio and listened intently as the news unfolded, with the ultimate pronouncement of Kennedy's death. We sat all day, continuing to listen for more news. At some point we made our way to the male volunteers' house to continue to discern what this moment meant. School had been cancelled. I walked by myself, and a student I did not know walked towards me with a sad face and stopped to say, 'This is wonderful'. I went through three translations in my head and realized that this was at least his third language, and by his face I knew he meant 'This is awful'. I thanked him and walked on. Later in the day, the governor, Mengeshu Seyoum invited us all to his palace to give his condolences. In the following days, in all my classes, I read President Kennedy's inaugural speech. At each class, I gave homework and left. It was difficult.

A few months later, Drs Ron and Phil decided to visit a Lutheran mission station as they had a very good clinic and health services. I travelled with them. We were warmly greeted and after touring their multiple work facility including a school and places for orphans, I asked them what their main work was as there were so many aspects to their activities. Without hesitation, one missionary said, 'to convert Coptic Christians to become Lutherans'. I was stunned. As a Lutheran from birth, who had seriously considered becoming a Lutheran missionary, I immediately knew I had made the right decision to join the Peace Corps, and thus ended my affiliation with any particular denomination. This important experience also opened my understanding that faith was too big and the various paths to redemption too many for any one religion to own.

We continued our work, taking excursions to various nature sites like waterfalls or up to Asmara to the big city for shopping and parties. Five of us took a hiking trip to a nearby village overnight. One of our students lived there and had prepared the families for our arrival. We were fed royally with good injera (a type of bread) and wat (chicken stew), and had a great night's sleep in our sleeping bags. We left in late morning and the weather had turned quite hot. We had drunk local wine the night before and so ended up drinking all of our water en route. I had fantasies of tomato juice during the whole hike. When we reached home we were so thirsty we drank at least 28 glasses of water apiece.

When my two-year commitment to the Peace Corps was up, I considered signing up for another year. I had also thought I would go into Public Health and study at the University of North Carolina. My two years of seeing a leper on our street corner every day showed me I could not face this kind of human tragedy. I applied for a job as a Student YWCA director and was accepted, sight unseen, at the University of Cincinnati.

Home through the Far East

Most of our Peace Corps volunteers were heading back home through Europe. A few of us decided to go back via the Far East. Two of us settled on India, Thailand, Vietnam, Singapore, the Philippines, Hong Kong, and Japan. We travelled light as many of our goods were shipped to the States. We also figured out how to land in the early evening in a place with no connecting flights until the following afternoon. Most airlines at that time then put you up in a hotel.

Our first stop was Bombay and the airlines put us up in the Taj Mahal Hotel. When we got to our room, it was so big that the beds looked the size of a postage stamp on a big envelope. We took a tour in the morning and then got our flight to New Delhi. We all did loads of shopping and sent things home. From there we boarded a train to Agra and spent a day marveling at the real Taj Mahal. We flew to Kashmir and stayed on a boathouse accompanied by rats on the floor during our two nights where we attempted sleeping. The mountains were spectacular. From there we visited the family of the two Indian teachers we had worked with in Makelle. Unfortunately, I drank some juice with ice at the marketplace, and I had stomach troubles for some time. The huge population of Calcutta floored us.

We went on to Thailand, visiting monuments and places of worship and meeting the lovely and very gentle folk. We then went to the island of Penang, just off the coast of Malaysia. This was a quiet time to be on long beaches. After that we went to Singapore for a short stop and onto the Philippines. There I went by myself north of Manila and stayed in a Peace Corps house. A typhoon arrived on the same day and I was marooned for three days, but as I had a flight to Hong Kong, I caught a bus back to Manila on that third day. Halfway to Manila, a bridge had been washed up. All of the passengers got out of the bus, and we climbed down a ladder on this riverbank, then crossed another ladder resting parallel to the river and up to the other side. There, a bus was waiting to take us to Manila.

Hong Kong is known for its shops of cloth and silks, so I went shopping again, but I had been met by a college friend and thus got a good tour. I met up again with my travelling companion and we stayed in a home when we arrived in Tokyo, Japan. We noticed that there were some huge hotels (like the Hilton) in the city. The US tourists would shop in the basement of these hotels, which were set up like 'markets'. Then they would go on an air-conditioned bus to go see the sites. It must have felt as if they had never left the States.

I felt at this time that I was experiencing moving from extreme poverty to more prosperous situations. Ethiopia was one of the poorest countries of the world, and slowly moving east, each country felt slightly more affluent than the one before. By the time I reached the States, I had been gradually acclimatizing to more prosperity. I had crossed the international date line, so arrived in the United States hours before I had left Japan. I had been invited to my college roommate's wedding in Kansas and raided the refrigerator for food in the middle of the night and fell asleep during the wedding.

Return cultural shock

After returning from my Far Eastern travel, I spent some time with my parents in Wisconsin. Then I drove my new red Volkswagen Beetle to Cincinnati. The former director of the student YW had paved the way for me to share an apartment with her ex-housemate, Pat Beanblossom, who was the head nurse of the ICU department at Cincinnati General Hospital. She was gracious, welcoming, and we hit it off fairly well. I was 24 years old when I took this job.

My main struggle that first year was return cultural shock. Although Pat lived modestly, I could not figure out how to deal with what was called 'trash'. For those two years in Ethiopia, every piece of scrap paper or tin can was saved and used again and again. I found myself getting angry, but did not think it appropriate to get angry at Pat. I just kept thinking that I should save everything, anything. We now know that recycling is a key element of reducing our footprint on this earth.

I arrived in Cincinnati before the students got there in September 1964. The chair of the Personnel Committee invited me to lunch in those first days. She suggested we eat on a river boat across the Ohio river in Kentucky. Halfway across the bridge, I said, 'Oh, sorry, I forgot to bring my passport!' She replied that I didn't need a passport to cross state lines. Having just hopped across many borders through the Far East, I was in the habit of always having my passport with me – this was a good laugh on me, and also reminded me that I was back in the States.

Having been the president of the student YWCA in college, I knew that students expected, rightfully so, to run their own organization. I saw my role as administering their decisions about programs, meetings, and projects. This was long before the days of the internet, so sending out notices, flyers, and organizing big mailings was a fun task. Scouting out opportunities in the communities in Cincinnati for projects and participating in campus ministry meetings further broadened my own awareness. The National YW was very focused on civil rights and so there were summer projects for voter registration in the South. I also found a Congregational Church in the African-American community in the West End. They ran after-school programs and welcomed college student volunteers. All of this felt more aligned with the YW and my own commitment to Civil Rights rather than focusing on pulling out of the Vietnam war.

About half of the 500 women members of this student YWCA were from sororities. Having had no experience with sororities and coming back from the poverty in Ethiopia, I felt quite alienated by the sorority/fraternity culture. All of the sororities/fraternities were segregated: separate white and black entities. I then started to research the legality of this practice. I spoke with law professors and university officials. The officials just said this 'was tradition' – which I did not accept.

I called the national YWCA staff about this and they sent a national YWCA staff person to visit our campus. Unbeknownst to me, Dorothy Height, from the National YW was also president of the National Council of Negro Women (a counterpart of the NAACP). I set up a public discussion with her with campus faculty and officials, as well as meetings with the students. She encouraged me to continue to advocate against segregated sororities/fraternities and I did this, but to no avail.

At the same time, our student YWCA board was made up of faculty women and wives of faculty members. The main task of the board was to raise funds. They held an annual international bazaar through a company that sent thousands of items for the pre-Christmas sale. The board was so well organized I just needed to 'be there'. Now that was a pleasure.

In this role, I sometimes found myself counselling students. This was new to me, and as a 'Leo' on my horoscope, my tendency is to give direct advice. After a number of years, I learned that asking questions and listening worked a wee bit better. As I was in the first year of the Peace Corps, a number of curious students came to ask about the Peace Corps and I remember at least a half dozen joined in later years.

In 1965, as the director of a student YWCA, I was invited to attend numerous regional and national student YWCA conferences. I was put in touch with Barbara Troxell, the director of the YW at Ohio Wesleyan University located near me. We often drove together to meetings in Chicago or the YM camp in Wisconsin. A deep friendship grew from these experiences, and Barbara was to visit me and my partner, Anne Hope, in Kenya and twice in South Africa later in our lives. In 1966, Barbara suggested I meet with some interesting Catholic women who had a center outside Cincinnati, called Grailville. I went with Barbara one time, and was fascinated. These were strong women with so much creativity and enthusiasm for life, as well as a deeply centered spiritual core. I went on to attend a number of programs at Grailville.

The YWCA at that time had training programs for many of us on group process. This was during the time of the National Training Laboratory (NTL) experimenting with how groups function and leadership styles within groups. Many of us in the YW were inspired by these participatory methods, which required a different form of leadership. This spurred me on to learn more where a key founder of NTL was a faculty member at Boston University. I was accepted onto the Adult Education Masters program and focused on organizational development and human relations.

During summer breaks from school time, I signed up to run workcamps in other places. I led about 12 students in a workcamp in Albuquerque, New Mexico, which was comprised mostly of younger girls getting out of a detention facility. These were not easy kids, but I found I could relate to their frustrations and was pleasantly surprised how well they took to games, and fun excursions. Another workcamp took me to Greece. With again about 12 men and women students, we travelled from the States to Geneva and through what was then Yugoslavia to Greece. We stayed in youth camps on the way. In Greece, we helped renovate a community center for the Greek Coptic Church.

Every morning I met with the Coptic priest for Greek coffee, which we finished in one swallow. I was learning about another culture, and ancient traditions.

When this workcamp was over, I took a one-week trip to a Greek island by myself and rented a room above a café on the Mediterranean Sea. What bliss. I walked the hills imagining the footsteps of ancient Greeks, swam in the warm water and ate grand food. For some reason I started to yearn for some news, but there were no English newspapers in this small town. I hopped a bus and went to the port city and got a newspaper. As I read it, I realized that most of the news was the same, just the countries where events happened were different. I find this lesson has stuck with me.

The following year, 1968, back in Cincinnati, I was recruited by an Episcopalian priest to join him in their campus ministry program. I had come to know this priest, Bill Hawley, and attended some classes with him. Process theology fascinated me. This goes back to evolutionary thought. Working with the campus ministry group left me free to pursue more civil rights activities, which were growing in intensity in 1968, and I began working in earnest with the coalition of black organizations. The War on Poverty program revitalized disenfranchised communities and new coalitions were formed. These were heady times with great hope. I worked closely with an Urban Ministries program that brought in community groups from Appalachia living in the inner city with black congregations. This reinforced a learning that the people at the base know best what they need.

Meanwhile, Bill Hawley, had received a grant in the summer of 1967 to send students to a workcamp in Dresden, East Germany. This was an exchange program between Coventry, England and Dresden, where in World War II, both of these cities were bombed with many civilians killed. The funds could accommodate five students with me as the leader. We met weekly throughout the school year learning German, the history of these two cities, and about the war. Just a few months before our departure, the East German government refused our visas for the workcamp. We were granted tourist visas for two weeks. Bill arranged that we would do two weeks' work on a hospital in Dresden that was still in ruins 20 years after the war. We then would go to a workcamp in Czechoslovakia, building a road with Russians and British students.

While in Dresden working alongside our student East German hosts, we were to sift out the rubble from the bombed-out hospital. We heard one evening of the riots in Detroit. The pent-up anger over civil rights had spread to the north, and I wondered what in hell I was doing in Dresden, going through the rubble of a war fought so long ago.

We then travelled to Czechoslovakia to Prague. A beautiful city indeed. We were met by a guide hired by the government; she was wonderful, though we felt a bit under scrutiny by the State. Then we travelled by train to Brno, Czechoslovakia. The work on the road was a mile or so away from the town. We engaged with the Russians a lot while working and of course at mealtimes. We also drank vodka with them in the evenings. They tried their best to have us drink alongside of them. Their method was: 'Cheers' and we clinked our glasses for the first drink. Then one would say, 'Everything comes in pairs, not alone'. So we clinked our second drink. Then another would say, 'There is only the Holy Trinity, and so we drink to the Holy Trinity'. Then another would say, 'Houses have four walls, so we drink to four walls'. And on and on it went. Well, one can imagine how we felt the next morning.

One of the Russians asked us, 'Why do you allow the Ku Klux Klan to continue in the United States?' This was a question we most likely had never encountered. I think we murmured something like the First Amendment about the right or associate with whomever and freedom of speech. Our answers seemed quite hollow and the question hung in the air.

The next year, the Soviets invaded Czechoslovakia on the very road we built. Now that felt rather odd to us when we met back on campus.

1968

On my return to Cincinnati, I resumed going to programs at Grailville. The Grailville program staff director, Audrey Sorrento, asked if I would like to be on their experimental semester program for college women called Semester at Grailville (SAG) in 1968. I was to find placements for SAG students one day a week in Cincinnati. I was also to participate in some of the learning sessions during the semester. My campus minister said yes. I had also applied to go to Boston University's Adult Education and Human Relations Department to get my Masters Degree. I was accepted for the next year and also decided to write a Masters thesis, which meant I would not have to take as many classes. I decided, with help from some professors, to conduct interviews of each SAG student before the semester started and give some tests. I would then conduct a similar interview and the same tests at the end of the semester. This would be the basis of my thesis – did SAG change the students' attitudes, behaviors, and thinking?

The SAG program started with no curriculum. The thirty-two students and eight of us mainly part-time staff, would meet together the first week to decide what we wanted to learn that semester. We then clustered into learning groups and staff were scattered in each cluster. I continued to want to learn more about group process so joined that group. Meanwhile, I found placements for students throughout Cincinnati for their day of volunteer work.

On 4 April 1968, Martin Luther King, Jr. was assassinated. This stunned us all. We had prayers, meditations, and time out of our schedule; this was most difficult for the black students amongst us, as they wished they were with their own families and communities. We struggled through the next month of SAG.

I did a final interview with each student and gave the tests again as I had done before the semester began. But I realized I had not set up a 'control' group. How did I know if the changes that might emerge from these before and after tests and interviews were because of the SAG program or because of the huge loss of Martin Luther King, Jr.? This was an important lesson for me.

In the summer of 1969, a student from Cincinnati named Sunny Robinson who had gone into the Peace Corps and been stationed in Ethiopia returned to the States. She then took on a workcamp in Puerto Rico and invited me to visit. I had very little money so she found a lovely guesthouse on the Caribbean Sea, which offered a small room if I would be a short order cook for breakfasts and lunches. Lovely. I would usually have about six customers each meal, not much work, so had time with Sunny and on the beach. Sunny had also invited me to share her apartment in Cambridge, while I studied at Boston University that September.

Upon returning to Cincinnati, I packed up all my belongings into my little red Volkswagen Beetle, and drove off to the east coast.

And then there was Anne

I had been told by several Grail members that another Grail member, a South African woman named Anne Hope, would also be enrolled in the same Masters program as myself. In my head I decided I didn't have time to be hostess to a white South African, so I would be polite, but that would be that. On the first day of class with Malcolm Knowles, I was reading a book by Michael Novak (then a progressive), called *Theology for Radical Politics*. A woman looked over my shoulder to see the title and I thought, oh, this might be Anne Hope. Malcolm came in and gave about a 40-minute lecture on participatory learning. When he asked for questions, I raised my hand and asked, 'Malcolm, why don't you practise what you preach?' He replied, 'We will do that next week.'

After class, Anne came up to me and after we introduced ourselves, she said, 'Well, that was very counter-dependent and one should never call a professor by his first name.' I responded by saying, 'We students have to keep these professors on their toes.' Anne and I then started talking; I offered her a ride home. I was intrigued. She said she was hunting for an apartment and had no car, so I offered to help her find one. Then a Grail member who lived near Boston University with her mother was searching for a new apartment. Anne and Mary Ann Kimball moved in together.

Anne and I saw each other often in classes. We went out to suppers, movies, plays, and found ourselves wanting to be with each other often. One day while I was parking my car near the Boston University bridge, I saw Anne walking across the bridge towards me. I stopped and realized I was falling in love with her. What sealed this for me was a few months later, I was picking up Anne and she was sobbing. I asked what had happened. She explained that many South Africans were being picked up by the South African police and interrogated, and some pushed out of the Security Police eleventh story windows to their death. I realized that her passion and empathy far exceeded mine, and this was the person I wanted to be with for the rest of my life, though how and where would be the challenge.

One of the performances we saw was the Utah Ballet company. One of the items was three couples dancing. One couple were totally focused on each other – face-to-face during the entire dance. A second couple were facing away from each other in opposite directions. A third couple were facing in the same direction and coming together at times to regain strength and intimacy. After this performance, Anne and I said to each other, we were that third couple. We had fallen in love.

When Anne had travelled to Boston, she had first stopped for a week in Portugal to be with Grail members there. They told her about this fantastic Brazilian educator, Paulo Freire, whose focus was on developing critical consciousness with peasants and the marginalized. Freire was scheduled to come to an Institute affiliated with Harvard that year. By wonderful chance, its director, Jim Lamb, was the husband of a Grail member, Joanne Lamb. Anne had known Joanne in her early days at Grailville. We both signed up for a one-year seminar with Freire. There will be more about his work later in this book.

Through my housemate, Sunny Robinson, Anne and I got in touch with a group called Community Change that was doing workshops on racism in white communities and churches. We joined them, which was helpful for us to put together the methods we were learning with Paolo Freire with what we were learning about participatory education. Community Change then was invited to work with the National YWCA board and we helped facilitate that workshop. The YWCA, through the leadership of Dorothy Height planned that at their next Assembly in 1970, they would introduce their One Imperative: 'to eliminate racism, wherever it exists, and by any means necessary.' This was during the period of the Black Panthers, and their slogan included 'by any means necessary', a phrase used by Stokely Carmichael, which was a red flag for a number of white folks in the YW. Anne and I were then invited to facilitate the caucus of white members prior to the YW convention.

While Anne and I worked on this white-on-white anti-racism training, we were linking the Freire method of critical consciousness with many participatory methods. We found that we worked well together, building on each other's ideas. In many ways, we were 'inventing' approaches that could be transformative on lots of levels: inside an individual, in teams and organizations, in the wider society and in our environment, this earth we share with all creatures and inhabitants.

Together, we found we had a common purpose in our lives. This purpose was social/economic/political transformation so that all of humanity would share our world in dignity, wealth, land, and power. The concern, of course, is how do you get there ….

At the same time, we discussed our process on anti-racism with Dr Knowles. He said it was too focused to one side – anti-racism, rather than being open-ended. We left our meeting with him and said no, he was wrong. After graduation, we went to a workshop led by Bob Terry, who also was working on anti-racism processes in the Midwest. Since we had developed some processes as well, we asked Bob if he would like to collaborate in writing a common book. We felt very strongly about not having a copyright so that local groups could use our materials freely without payment. Bob turned us down. We then made a booklet called *White-on-White: an anti-racism manual for facilitators*. This was passed on from facilitator to facilitator from 1971 forward. God only knows if any exist now.

That same summer a friend of Anne's and mine offered us use of her cabin in Tabernash, Colorado just outside Denver. We drove across very windy prairies of Nebraska and finally arrived. For the first time, we had a space for ourselves. We talked, we read our books and shared our common understanding of the meaning of life. We drove back at summer's end to Boston where Anne began courses at the Episcopal Divinity School and other courses at Harvard. I had been asked to join the National staff of the student YWCA to deliver white-on-white anti-racism workshops to colleges throughout the USA. This was hectic for me, as I travelled at least every other week to a different part of the USA. At some point, someone asked me, 'Where do you live, Sally?' And the first thing that popped into my head was 'seat 6A', which was the seat I always requested. No end of laughter at that revelation.

The second semester in 1971, Anne joined the Semester at Grailville staff near Cincinnati. I was able to arrange my flights to stop for a few days to be with her. At this time, Anne was trying to get a work permit for me to enter South Africa. At this same time, there was a global boycott of Polaroid, as these were the cameras used in South Africa for identity documents, which excluded black and so-called 'colored' people from what the 'whites' considered their territory. Anne tried many different ways, including through a lawyer friend of hers, but I kept on being turned down to enter South Africa. The South African government must have known about my involvement in the Polaroid boycott.

I was still travelling coast to coast doing anti-racism training at various colleges and universities. When Anne was free, I would invite her to staff with me. That summer, Anne and I facilitated workshops on the west coast, and took a trip up to Vancouver, Canada to see some of Anne's cousins. I found Vancouver and its surroundings wonderfully beautiful. We then went to the University of Wisconsin to help facilitate a national meeting of the student YWCA. The YW had just voted earlier to adopt the One Imperative: to eliminate racism, wherever it exists and by any means necessary. Our main job was to make sure everyone was heard, and their opinions/thoughts respected and taken in to build a common understanding for the YW in the future. The second night we were there, about 3 or 4 a.m. a bomb went off on campus that shook the windows and buildings of the YMCA residence where we were staying. This rather large bomb had been placed in a laboratory that was doing research for the US Defense Department. This was at the height of the Vietnam war.

Interestingly, Anne was sleeping next to the outside wall of our room, and I was sleeping next to the inside wall. We both jumped out of our beds, and Anne ran to the inside wall, and I ran to the outside wall to go look out of the windows. Anne yelled at me, get back to the inside wall. Typical of me to want to see everything going on! After several minutes, all of our YW delegates were in the halls. As we were so focused on racism, many of us conjectured that we might have been the target of the attack. Later we found that one person had been killed, and that the bomb was set to go off on a timer at 4 a.m. when it was expected no one would be in the laboratory, which was doing work for the Pentagon and the Vietnam War effort. Our debriefing from this experience was intense, and by the end of the meeting, a deeper understanding of our experience was reached.

At the beginning of September 1971, Anne and I facilitated a workshop at Oberlin College to which we had been invited by Nancy Richardson, who was the director of the student YW. Anne's US visa was about to run out. She had booked her ticket back to South Africa from a nearby airport. I still did not have a work permit to enter South Africa. At this moment, I felt I needed to make a critical decision regarding whether I would work politically in Cincinnati, or follow Anne to South Africa. Nancy listened to me endlessly during this time.

During that past year, we had also been looking for funding for me to work in South Africa. We heard about a church program sponsored by the Presbyterian and Methodist national churches for a program called Frontier internship. We had talked with the director, Margaret Flory, about our difficulties of getting a visa for me to be in South Africa. They had scheduled a 3-week program with Paulo Freire in Geneva, Switzerland in September and Margaret said I should still go to this program. I jumped at the chance. I packed my bags for the 3-week trip. Freire had pulled together a fantastic team from Brazil to work with him. The 15 or so Frontier Interns learned much about Freire's approach as well as the socio-political-economic analysis of the countries we would be engaging.

Five days before this program finished, I got a call from Anne in South Africa. She had gone to Swaziland, a land-locked country by South Africa and got a position for me to work with the Adult Education Department at the University of Swaziland. This department was working with a local literacy organization, called Sabenta, and UNESCO, to implement a national literacy program. They would welcome both of us to work with them. I would work full-time and Anne half-time, as she was also working with the Christian Institute in Johannesburg, South Africa.

I immediately said yes and went and purchased a typewriter. The Swiss keyboard, however, had different positions for some of the keys. I actually used this typewriter for about twenty years, including typing the three volumes of *Training for Transformation* manuscripts for the publisher 12 years later. I hopped on an airplane to Portugal and on to Mozambique where Anne picked me up. She drove me to Swaziland where she had found a house. We met the director of the Adult Education Department, Ross Kidd, and the staff of Sabenta.

Personalities and principles

Anne and I had very different personalities and styles. Anne was very gracious, a listener, and had deep compassion for anyone she met. At the same time, she had a backbone of steel if she felt others did not understand her wider purpose. On the other hand, I have this need to 'be productive', to get things done. I didn't mind making mistakes, as those were to be learned from and I would just try another way to get to the aims. When Anne and I took the Myers-Briggs test on personalities, Anne tested more as an introvert, feeling, intuitive, and as a perceiver (one who takes in many ideas and is not too worried about making a decision soon). I would come to trust Anne's intuitions most of the time. She was often 'right' about spotting future leaders in groups. She would see the whole of something and synthesize its meaning in simple language. For example, she was able to summarize the key principles of Freire into six points in simple English that continue to be used globally.

I regret I never asked Anne how she did that. I suspect this came from her daily morning meditations and readings in depth. For the 46 years I was with Anne, she would wake up early each morning and read serious works for two hours, then meditate for a half hour and do yoga for another half hour. By 7 a.m. she was ready for breakfast. As I stumbled out of bed she would often say quite chirpily, 'time for breakfast'. I learned over time to ask Anne to summarize what she had read that morning. This was a wonderful way for me to understand the depths of new thinking, on economics, geo-political struggles, liberation or feminist theologies, and the list could go on. When we worked in groups, a participant might say something and I would quickly see a link to something Anne had read. I would turn to Anne and ask if she could share what she had read about what had just been posed by this participant. Anne would often be able to recite what she had read by heart. What a gift, and one I would never achieve. When Anne would present a theory or have an input in a workshop, she was succinct, clear, and everyone listened very closely.

On the other hand, on the Myers-Briggs test I tested more as an extrovert, thinker, sensate (practical) and one who came to judgement (or need for closure). I found when I was working in another country, I was much more a 'feeler' as I learned I could never truly 'think' through another culture; I had to 'feel' it. A constant issue between Anne and myself was that I wanted to make decisions quickly, while Anne ruminated the possibilities. I learned how to coax her early before a decision had to be made so she would have enough time to go through a thousand options before we had to decide. Well, that is probably an exaggeration, but as someone who wanted to come to a decision then and there, it felt like she had a thousand options rumbling in her head.

Another amusing difference between us was that Anne would be thinking about a project or an idea and would share that with me. A few days later I would share with her that I had a proposal written, and thought I could find three or four funders, so we could start that work in a few months. Anne's horrified reply would be something like, 'Sally, that was just an idea. I didn't mean we have to do it!'

This interplay between our personalities, styles, and love multiplied our ability to both persevere and become more creative.

The Freire method is sometimes called the psycho-social method. With Anne being more introverted, it also meant she worked with understanding herself through therapy and getting a graduate degree in counselling. She looked deeply into the psychology of a person by listening intently. I focused more on the socio/political nature of the work of an organization or teamwork. I was also a keen problem-solver.

For those who may not know much about Paulo Freire's approach to education, I will share here what we adapted over time of his work. Here are the six principles that Anne developed.

a. *The aim of education is radical transformation*

For the marginalized of the world, 'the way things are' is not satisfactory, and it is not the only way they can be. Transformative education is based on the hope that it is possible to change life for the better. It must be based on the vision of a new, more just society. 'Radical' means going to the roots. The cause of much of the unnecessary suffering in the modern world lies deep in the values which influence modern industrial/technological 'civilization'. This 'civilization' influences most of the world. These dominant 'values' for material possessions and power are paramount.

To transform society we need to tap into much deeper values of cooperation, justice, and concern for the common good. Most faith traditions constantly challenge us to live according to these different values which are essential aspects of love. **That is why transformative education is essentially a spiritual process.**

b. *Relevant-generative themes: empowerment*

Everybody thinks the education they provide is relevant, but who decides what is relevant to a particular community? Many have stressed that the community themselves must choose the issues which are central in their education and development programs. Paulo Freire has taken this concept much deeper, by pointing out the link between emotion and motivation to act. He calls these 'generative themes' – or concerns that generate life – movement to action and not apathy.

c. *Dialogue*

Dialogue is crucial in every aspect of participatory learning, and in the whole process of transformation. The challenge to build a just society, based on equality, is very complex. We have learnt to believe that there are experts who have all the knowledge we need to know. For years traditional education has been seen as a process of passing on information from one 'person who knows' (the teacher) to others 'who do not know' (the pupils). Freire refers to this process as 'banking' education, as the teacher makes regular deposits in the empty mind of the pupil.

Now we find that on a great many issues, the so-called 'experts' have been wrong. This is particularly so in the field of development, where again and again the advice of outside 'experts' has led to greater poverty. Of course, many have valuable information to contribute; we need dialogue to draw in the insights of all who are concerned as we search for solutions. Local participation is crucial for effective development. There is a role for information from those who have special knowledge or experience. A group is far more likely to absorb and benefit from this input through dialogue which brings to the surface all the latent questions in their minds. Relevant information then challenges participants to deeper thinking and further dialogue. **Dialogue requires patience, humility and a real belief that there is something that one can learn from the other person.** The role of the animator is to create a climate in which true dialogue can take place.

d. Problem-posing and the search for solutions

Once we have found the generative issues of a community, we need to find a concrete way of presenting a familiar experience of the core problem back to the group. Freire called these 'codes' which were posters, plays, photographs, songs and simulation games. With a good code, the animator does not have to explain the problem. Through critical questions, the animator helps the group go as deeply as possible into root causes and challenges them to find solutions for themselves.

e. Reflection and action

The animator provides a situation in which people can stop their daily occupations and reflect critically on what they are doing. A code helps enormously to speed up the process. The groups identify any new information or skills they need, get this information and/or training, and then plan action. Often initial plans of action may solve some aspects of a problem, but not deal deeply enough with the root causes.

By setting a regular cycle of reflection and action, groups become more and more capable of effectively changing their situations.

f. No education is neutral

No teacher is ever fully 'objective'. We are all conditioned by our life experiences and it is important that we look critically at how these have affected our values and our judgments. We need to check to what extent we use our role and our power in the group to try and shape others in our own image. We also need to look to what extent we encourage participants to develop along their own unique paths. We also need to see to what extent our education is 'domesticating' participants to fit into the role required of them by the dominant culture, and to what extent it is liberating them to be critical, creative, free, active and responsible members of society – as well as in this learning group. For example, whether malnutrition is 60 per cent or 64 per cent is a fact, but this information, put next to increased spending on weapons and less money for nutrition in a country's budget, changes our understanding of the causes of malnutrition radically.

'**Problem-posing education is prophetic, and as such is hopeful, corresponding to the historical nature of human beings. It affirms people as beings who transcend themselves, who move forward and look ahead…. For whom looking at the past must only be a means of understanding more clearly what and who they are, so that they can more wisely build the future.**'

Paul Freire
Pedagogy of the Oppressed, p. 57

Two of these principles were key for me. The first was that education is not neutral. Either you were on the side of the oppressed or not. This is the lens through which you saw/see the world. The second principle was like being on a balcony and trying to see the wider picture. Is the generative theme for this moment gender, economic inequity, land, or housing? Most likely it would be all of them, but asking which was burning in the culture at this particular moment.

Getting down to work

'Every best practice is based on sound theory'

One of the Sabenta staff took us on a field trip to meet local community groups. This was to give us an orientation of the types of people whom the literacy program would serve. One was a group of more than 100 women. Through an interpreter, the women talked with much passion about how they were being abused or oppressed by their husbands and men in general. We had been fairly in touch with the feminist movement in the States in our anti-racism work, but these testimonies were so graphic and strong, we knew this issue of violence against women needed to be addressed. However, we also knew that Swaziland was a 'kingdom' ruled by a king who had over 100 wives. There was a huge prohibition on discussing women's rights and freedoms. We kept our thoughts to ourselves.

Anne came every other week to Swaziland while I continued to work mainly with the Sabenta literacy team. This team brought together 20-30 community leaders whom we trained to do listening surveys. These listening surveys were not for the leaders to ask questions but rather to listen in places where people talked freely about what they had strong feelings about. Such locations could be barber shops, standing in line for buses, or at the water wells. After a few months, we gathered together to name these concerns, categorize them by themes, and generated one word that represented that theme. We also worked on questions. This entire process is written up in Book 1 of *Training for Transformation*. It is an exciting process and with about 30 themes and words, it is possible for an illiterate person to write their own language with words and sentences. This is possible in pairs of participants finding consonants and vowel clusters to put together to form a word like *ku li ma*.

These themes were put into posters that posed the problem and questions developed for the animator to use for discussions in the literacy classes. A lot of preparation was needed before the training of the literacy teachers. Once the Sebenta team was ready with the materials, they also recruited about 100 literacy teachers from throughout the country. Anne and I worked with the team for this training, and all of the work took about eight months.

During this first training workshop, Anne was up at the front of the room giving some background on these methods. I was standing in the back of the room. Suddenly behind me were two Swazi policemen. They asked me where was Anne Hope. I said she was giving the lecture and pointed to her. It was close to a break for tea. I went to Anne to say the police were here and wanted to talk to her. We looked into each other's eyes, and went to the police. They handed Anne a letter stating that she had to be out of Swaziland in two days. We were astounded. We went to the director of Sabenta, and others picked up the training as we went home.

At home, Anne and I just kept asking why this was happening. Earlier, we had invited South Africans to come to Swaziland to learn more about these methods, and had wondered if the Swazi police knew about this. Just before this workshop with South Africans, we were told we could not hold this workshop. While we were thinking through why Anne was being thrown out of the country, Anne remembered that the Catholic Bishop of Swaziland was a relative of a Grail member. We then went to Bishop Zwane and told him our story. Bishop Zwane knew many of the government cabinet members and said he would try to find out why Anne was being thrown out. He reported that the cabinet had discussed us and said that we were a plot of the World Council of Churches to train guerrillas to overthrow the South African apartheid government. We smiled and said to ourselves that we wished that we could have done the latter.

More importantly, we realized that there must have been a South African government informant at the World Council of Churches. When Anne was returning to South Africa, she went via Geneva to the World Council of Churches to discuss with Paulo Freire our intentions to implement these methods in southern Africa. Paulo was now on the World Council of Churches' educational staff. Anne had a two-hour lunch with Paulo. As noted earlier, I had been in Paulo's seminar at the World Council for three weeks. A number of years later we found out that the head of the Swaziland police was a South African whose name was Colonel Roache. We often chuckled at his name and jokingly called him cockroach.

Anne packed and left. We then arranged to meet in Mozambique, as I could not get into South Africa. I described earlier how we had been followed and how I went back to Swaziland.

Upon my return from Mozambique, I received a letter from the Swazi government, stating that I was a prohibited immigrant and giving me two weeks to leave. A Grail member from Johannesburg came to Swaziland to help pack up what little household goods we had accumulated during our nine months' work. Anne still had her passport, so we met again in Mozambique and headed up the Indian Ocean coast to a small park on a lagoon. There we rented a small roundoval (a traditional hut in a nature reserve) with two tiny beds and a small table in between the two beds. There was a small one-foot square window on one side.

That first day we spent some time on the beach, picking up stones and shells to make a chess game with the board made by hand in the sand. That evening, having bought a kerosene burner to cook food and boil water for tea and coffee, a storm started to grow into a typhoon. For two days the typhoon raged. We sat in our roundoval, and played chess and tried to read with what little light came in from the tiny window - which we had to cover with a towel because of the fierce winds and water. On the third day of the typhoon, it finally occurred to us that the most comfortable place in which to sit and have some light was our car! So we drove down to the lagoon side and read *Jonathan*

Livingstone Seagull while watching the huge waves and listening to classical music on our tiny cassette player. Pure bliss!

When the typhoon had moved on, we caught a boat to take us out of the lagoon to walk on the ocean side. The pounding breakers looked quite dangerous to this small-town girl, but Anne reveled in it. We then went back to the city to say our goodbyes. Anne drove back to Johannesburg and I waited a day to pick up my flight to Johannesburg, and then flew on to Kenya, Egypt, the World Council of Churches in Geneva, and finally back to the United States.

Anne and I had been told separately that we could be with each other at the Johannesburg Airport where I changed planes. When I landed, I went to the exit and there she stood. She was arguing with the customs officials on her side of the barrier as I was arguing with those on my side of the barrier. Neither of us had any luck. We found a place where there was thick glass separating the two areas but we could not hear each other. I saw a public phone booth near me and quickly copied down its phone number, showing it to Anne through the glass. She went to a phone booth near her and called me. We talked for a good length of time. Then we hung up our phones, not knowing if we would ever be together again. Anne wrote a poem about this experience and part of it reads:

> To preserve white wealth and power
> They've made a concrete glassy world
> Where human hearts are trampled
> And hands of love are broken
> Where properties and prices rise resplendent,
> And persons shrink and perish …
> Is this the price we proudly pay?

On my way back to the States

Anne's sister, Joan, and her family lived in Nairobi, Kenya. Joan's husband, Jimmy, was head of the English department at the University of Nairobi. I stayed with them a few days and even had a chance to play tennis with Joan. That helped me to understand Joan and her relation to Anne in a different way, which was lovely. She beat me but graciously, as Anne sometimes did! I planned to go to Egypt to meet with the Grail International President, Simone Tagher, an Egyptian. I went to the Egyptian Embassy to get a visa and asked about any shots I would need. The visa went through quickly and was told I did not need any shots to enter.

Upon landing in Cairo, at the immigration desk, I was told in no uncertain terms that I needed a cholera shot to enter Egypt. I argued and argued. But I had no luck. They said I could get a cholera shot but had to be in quarantine and they would take me there. They bundled me up to a site in the desert that looked like an old army barracks. Fortunately I had Simone's telephone number and I called her from this site. She got directions and came to a lone palm tree along a very high barbed wire fence. I had grabbed a chair and walked to Simone and sat on my side of the fence. We talked for hours, eating some of the food she had brought along. We did this for 3 days. Meanwhile, I stayed in a very small room and slept on the cot provided and ate food from their canteen. I asked at least three times a day when we would get our cholera shots, and was always told, 'Oh, it is coming soon.' After the third day, Simone and I decided that those shots would not materialize, so I booked myself on an airplane to Geneva. From there I flew to Paris to a Grail Center.

I wanted to tell Paulo Freire's team and Paulo himself that there must be a South African informant at the World Council. How did they know that Anne had had a two-hour lunch with Paulo and that I had been on his course for three weeks? The best I could do was alert them to our suspicions.

I stayed in Paris for a few days and took in the sights as well as being with Grail friends, as this was important to me. One day I visited the Eiffel Tower and spent some time in the parks. Near the end of that afternoon I noticed a man who seemed to be following me. When I hopped on the metro, the man entered the same car. When I changed trains, he also changed again onto the same train car. When I got off at my station, he followed. The Grail Center was about three blocks away. He started gaining ground on me. I turned around and ordered him to stop following me. He continued. I stopped, grabbed his arm, and swung around with my right hand and punched him as hard as I could on the chin. I walked on and turned around about a block later. I saw him still holding his chin. That guy certainly felt all of my pent-up anger about all that had happened to me in Swaziland, South Africa and Egypt. I then flew onto the States.

I was met at the Boston airport by my good friends, Nancy Richardson and Sunny Robinson. As they were dealing with my luggage, other friends saw us and greeted me. Later they would ask Nancy, 'Was Sally tortured? She looks like it.' And in many ways, I was … I can only imagine how physical torture might be even more damaging to the soul.

Nancy and Sunny took me on a travelling holiday up to the Cody Institute in Nova Scotia, where a friend from Swaziland was studying. We then meandered through Canada down to Cincinnati, Ohio where I would stay at the Grail Center there for several months.

Time to heal

In the warm sun of summer at Grailville, I took time to read and carry out some chores, including painting the front door of our meditation building, called the Oratory. This is a splendid barn converted into a worship area with oak floors, and a very high ceiling, which is the original roof of the barn. The old beams are still in place, as is a ceiling-roof skylight that comes down to the altar. A Grail artist, Ginger Legato, had designed the painting that would go on the outside of the front door for me to follow during the actual painting of the door. I got to work. Of course, being a Tom Sawyer type, when friends would come to have a chat with me, I passed them my brush and sat down to supervise, just like 'Tom'. All this was done in good humor.

Although I had known the Grail for ten years, I had not joined. My relationship with Anne was so strong, however, that at this time I felt a way to be close to her, even at a distance, would be to join the Grail. I met with the leadership of the National USA Grail for discernment. They asked if I was willing to be a responsible member and I said yes. A few us of later wondered if there were 'irresponsible members', and we had a good chuckle. Grail members held a ritual in honor of my membership, which included an older member, Audrey Schomer, singing 'There is a balm in Gilead'; so appropriate for my feelings of my loss of Anne at this time.

Another Grail member lived in Philadelphia and knew of a group working on campaigns on the local and state level. This put me in touch with some great organizers, and gave me the opportunity to do some research on foundations who worked on similar issues as I learned how to craft funding proposals to local and state needs. A few months later, it looked like Anne would be able to leave South Africa so I went to Boston to be with friends there while waiting for her call telling me where to meet her once she left South Africa.

Transitions mean flexibility

Anne and I talked on the phone numerous times despite our rather stilted conversations, as we were sure the South African government was tapping her phone. Anne had already been warned that her days of freedom were numbered, as so many of the people she had been working with in the black consciousness movement were being picked up by the police and interrogated. She knew she would either be arrested or banned. She had a choice of awaiting the realization of those possibilities or of voluntarily going into exile. She met with a support group and decided to go into exile - but she had no passport.

Anne explained this to her mother and lamented that if only she had an Irish grandparent she could leave legally, as the Irish government was offering Irish passports to those working against apartheid. Anne's mother said, 'But you do, Anne, your grandmother was born in Ireland'. Anne argued that her grandmother was from Canada. Her mother explained that her grandmother had moved to Canada when she was two years old, but she had been born in Ireland. The work then began to collect all the documents of birth and marriage certificates of grandparents, parents and of course her own. The trick, however, turned out to be that her great-grandfather was in the British Army, which was occupying Ireland at that time. On the form, Anne wrote that her great-grandfather was an 'Officer'. Anne's mother told Anne to be more specific and write British Army Officer, but Anne said that they could think it was just any kind of 'officer'. All the papers were sent to Ireland and months later Anne received a new birth certificate with the occupation of her great-grandfather listed as 'gentleman'. This was a lovely story we told often, and it always elicited a good chuckle.

Once she had her Irish passport, Anne gathered up her belongings and booked a ticket out of the country for a Friday. She went to the airport a day early to avoid being stopped from leaving South Africa. She flew to Malawi where her sister, Joan, now lived. Arriving in Malawi, Anne called Joan and when Joan picked up the phone Anne said, 'This is Anne'. Joan's reply was 'Anne who?' Anne realized that being in exile would mean she would not be 'known'. This question would haunt her over and over again, questioning 'Where do I belong?'

Joan gave Anne contacts with Maryknoll Sisters in Tanzania and Kenya where she might find a place to work. Anne went to Tanzania. With the help of the Maryknoll Sisters she found that the Tanzanian government already had a literacy program that was using 'functional literacy' that trained people into jobs and basic reading and writing. As we both were very supportive of Nyerere's socialist government, we would later agree that this was not the right place to add the Freire methods of critical consciousness. This might start a 'competition' with an already established government literacy program.

Anne then travelled to Kenya to be met by Sr Janice McLaughlin and was introduced to Enda Byrne, the director of the Catholic Bishop's Conference Development Department. Enda and Anne got on famously. Enda totally agreed with the Freireian approach to development and invited Anne, with me, to come work in Kenya. But first, we would have to write a funding proposal to a Catholic agency in Germany called Misereor.

Coming together in Greece

Anne and I had arranged that we would meet in Greece when she left Kenya. As I had been in Greece earlier, I suggested we go to an island to catch up with each other. On that island, Anne shared that we could go to Kenya to work with the Bishop's Development Department to train diocesan groups on community development. This was a surprise to me; however, as she had gone into exile, it only seemed fair we go to Kenya. We discussed our proposal, which we would send to Misereor in Germany. We found the only bank on the island that had a typewriter with our script. Anne then wrote our proposal page by page, dashed down to the bank where the staff had set me up with paper and carbon paper. I worked on the budget. Anne's proposal was in the form of a poem and quite persuasive. The bank staff were intrigued by our process and we were given coffee as we worked. We proceeded to send off our proposal to Misereor.

At the same time, we telephoned Simone Tagher, the international president of the Grail at that time, asking her to come to Greece for us to brief her about Anne's status now as being in exile and our future work in Kenya. On the day she was due to arrive, we went by ferry to the Athens' airport to welcome her. We waited and waited. No Simone. We then started searching every nook and cranny of the airport – no Simone. We finally gave up and went back to our island. When we telephoned Simone to find out what was happening, it transpired she had sent a telegram to a different island to say she could not come due to illness and we should come to Egypt. Anne and I arranged to fly to Cairo.

In Cairo, we stayed at the international secretariat of the Grail. We had many talks with Simone, and she took us on a number of tours and we also went on public transportation to markets and to the city. One evening, Simone said she would take us to the pyramids as they were more interesting at night. After a very late-night supper at a restaurant on the Nile River, we drove out to the pyramids. They were spectacular, but it was freezing cold. When we drove to the Sphinx, where according to legend Napoleon had shot off the nose, I whispered to Anne that I was so cold I couldn't see a thing!

We flew on to Geneva, Switzerland to the World Council of Churches to discuss with Paulo Freire our extension of his work. We also wanted to brief him about the situation in southern Africa. Paulo, was his usual, hospitable self, and we enjoyed his company and his blessings. After that we went on to Cincinnati to be at the Grail Center. The Grail program team had set up a meeting with a priest working in Mexico with Grail members there adapting Freire's methods. This added another layer of experience and understanding of this important approach to community empowerment. Anne and I then drove to Cornwall-on-Hudson, New York, with several other Grail members for a 4-day workshop Anne and I facilitated on putting Freire's methods into practice.

Two events from this time remain with me. As we were driving in the August heat, Anne suggested we find a place to swim, to rest and cool off. We saw a sign to a lake, so we turned off the highway and came to a barrier where a guard was collecting money to go to the lake. Now, with our deeply critical consciousness in high gear, we said to the guard, we shouldn't have to pay to swim in the lake, as this was God's creation. The guard replied, no, this was Mr Jones's creation - it was a man-made lake.

During this workshop on Freire's methods, we had small groups work on the question: 'You are the state legislature and have the power to make this the most equitable and livable state in the country. What are the key elements you would implement?' The purpose of this exercise was to enable people to articulate their values and focus on what areas of advocacy they would like to pursue in the future. After long discussions, one group brought back a suggestion that broke us all up in tears of laughter. That group reported back that one of their ten or more concerns was what to do with accumulated trash. Their solution was to dump it in the neighboring state. Of course, that doesn't work; however, in hindsight, this 1973 proposal was prophetic.

After this workshop and visiting with friends in Boston, we flew on to London. Anne's childhood friend, Maire Pompe, with whom Anne had kept in close contact, welcomed us. She had worked in an international Catholic organization called Pax Romana where Anne had been a vice-president. A colleague of Maire's, Jurgen Nikolai, was now the head of the African department of Misereor, the German funder that had agreed to support our upcoming work in Kenya. Maire invited Jurgen to come for a day to meet us in person. After hours of discussion with Jurgen and his colleague, Agnes Billing, they became good friends and would become supporters of our future work. We did not realize at the time that this support and friendship would last until the days of my writing this - 45 years later.

Kenya: the Camelot years

On our flight to Kenya, the pilot of the plane announced there had been a military coup in Chile. Neither of us had ever heard a pilot give news to the passengers before a flight, and I never did in the future either. This was sad news.

When we arrived in Nairobi, we were met by Sr Janice and taken to a Catholic guest house to rest up, before we were whisked off to meet with Enda Byrne at the Catholic Secretariat. Over the next few weeks, we continued to meet with Enda to set up some national workshops and arranged interviews with the Council of Churches staff, and other Protestant clergy. At the same time, we agreed that the place where Sr Janice and three other women religious groups were living would be ideal for our new home. Jamhuri Estate was a large housing estate with over 500 townhouses occupied by Kenyans and the rent was affordable. We went to auctions to furnish our new home, but during our time there, we never had a refrigerator; we were very close to a shopping area where we could get milk and other perishables several times a week.

We had arrived in 1973 with a national election coming up soon. One of the rivals to Jomo Kenyatta had a slogan that said: '10 great years where 10 million beggars created 10 millionaires'. At that time, the population of Kenya was 10 million people. Jomo Kenyatta was accumulating wealth and his wife, Mama Ngina, was setting up charcoal businesses that were depleting the environment so quickly that desertification was becoming a growing problem. The leader of the opposition to such practices was later found murdered in a nearby forest in Nairobi.

We settled in and started giving workshops on development, participatory processes and communications. This produced immediate invitations from groups around the country, mostly from Catholic dioceses and parishes. One diocese wanted to initiate a literacy campaign. We then went to Kitui numerous times to train a team in the Freire method, starting with listening surveys to find generative themes. What was meant by Freire about 'generative themes' was identifying what people had strong feelings about. The survey teams would not ask local folks directly what they felt about x, y, or z, but just listen in key spots where people talked freely: bus stops, in buses, at the barber shop, or the borehole where women collected water for their families. In the next workshop we gathered the themes, put them in order of a key word in the local language (like farming, reading, school, land, etc.). We also asked the group to describe a scene to represent these themes. These descriptions would then be drawn by an artist. The process for adapting Freire's work can be found in the *Training for Transformation Handbooks* (Vol 1-3). These books were published 10 years after our work and based on real work with groups and projects.

In addition, we were asked to run training programs at the Institute of Adult Learning at the University of Nairobi. Just at that time, a new staff person there, Thelma Awori, who was originally a Liberian married to a Ugandan, was very interested in the Freireian approach. We asked her and two other Institute staff members to do co-training with us on some national workshops. Thelma became a big advocate of our work when a number of years later she became the Deputy Director of UNIFEM (the women's division of the United Nations) and then the deputy to Kofi Annan, the General Secretary of the United Nations.

A notable experience was a workshop we implemented with the National Christian Council of Churches. The director, John Kamau, was in attendance along with his deputy, Bethul Kiplagat who later became the Foreign Minister for the Kenyan government. Kiplagat also did some co-training with us on national programs. During this workshop, we used a simulation game called 'Star Power'. The group was divided into three unequal groups of participants – from large numbers to quite small. In this trading game, the rich get richer and the poor poorer. During the game, many times the 'poor' in large numbers coalesce with the middle class and start a revolution of sorts. After the game, we spend time debriefing the simulation with participants describing what happened, and if and how this happens in real life. The participants were very clear that this is how the poor have very little say or political power in the game and there are little to no alternatives through which to change the game (read system). John Kamau, the director, stopped the discussion and said that this was totally unrealistic, that the army would step in and stop any actions to change how this system works. He then said, there would be no more workshops with Anne and me. Quite a blow. Of course, the more progressive members of his staff continued to come to some workshops, but opportunities for building local alliances between Catholic diocesan initiatives and the Council of Churches were now limited. The way around this however, was working with the large All African Council of Churches and national Protestant denominations, which we did. We later learned that John Kamau was the owner of quite a few large buildings and companies in Nairobi.

Anne and I continued to receive more and more invitations to do workshops for dioceses and also for doing specific work on developing literacy campaigns in local languages. We then decided we needed a longer training program for the volunteers and some Kenyan diocesan staff. We developed a four-week phased program called DELTA (Development Education and Leadership Teams in Action). These four one-week sessions were spread out over a year with two months in between each residential session, to allow participants to practise what they had just learned. The four phases were: looking at key issues and participatory methods; leadership styles and how group processes worked; organizational development; and social/economic/political structures of society. We believed it was better to cover the political issues on the last phase as it could be the most controversial. Each of these phases had spiritual reflections and meditations to ground the work into one's deepest values and build long term commitment. We were lucky to have some members of the Institute for Adult Studies at the University of Nairobi working with us.

For the DELTA program, we asked each diocese to send five participants. We asked that there be at least two women in each team. A number of them were volunteers and so we had to work the schedule around school holidays and the like. When we received the names of potential participants, we found there was usually only one woman on the team. We asked why. And the answers were usually, 'Well, the women are not ready for this yet'. We didn't buy this, but we went ahead with DELTA.

After the second year into the DELTA program, Anne and I decided, in consultation with other women in DELTA, to start a separate women's three-week phased program called WINDOW: Women in the National Development of Women. We knew that women were the weavers of the social fabric of communities. WINDOW drew women in many fields including primary health care, women's small businesses, organizing market women and parish women leaders. These women soon were drawn into diocesan employment.

Some of these women in WINDOW also wanted a weekend to understand the Grail, the international movement in which Anne and I were both members. This happened near the end of our stay in Kenya, but these women persisted and we sent three of them to Portugal for a workshop on the Grail.

By this time, we were stretched beyond our capacity. We had hired a woman who knew the Grail in Uganda, Mary Busharizi, to be an administrator, but we needed a team of trainers. We then hired Joseph Ikalur and convinced Enda Byrne to join this team as development and parish trainers. We hired Adelina Mwau and Sr Becky Macugay (a Maryknoll Sister) to enable dioceses to implement literacy programs. We also hired a Dutch agricultural specialist and then Sr Leah Wambui to work with the women's groups. This obviously meant we needed to find a much bigger office.

Several Tanzanians had come to some of these workshops in Kenya. Some invited Anne and me to give a workshop in Arusha (in northern Tanzania). At that time the border between Kenya and Tanzania was closed, and US AID was sponsoring this workshop for government community development workers; they assured us they would get permission for us to drive and have a permit to cross the border. That permission did not come. They then sent us air tickets. The cost difference was $50 for us to drive and $5,000 to fly us. This was at the United States taxpayers' expense. We had to fly from Nairobi to Kigali, to Dar es Salaam, to Arusha. But as we wanted to visit the Grail in Tanzania, we decided to go.

Once we got there, we found the head of US AID had been the head of 'villageization' of rural areas in Vietnam during the war, a way to contain local people to be on the USA side of that war. Besides this, the workshop was for government workers and at that time, the President of Tanzania was Julius Nyerere, a practical socialist who was beloved by the people. The US AID organizers had arranged this workshop in a very plush hotel with an open bar. A great learning for me was that no matter the content of the workshop to empower local people to control their own destinies, the big message was for these workers to aspire to greater privileges and wealth for themselves.

After the workshop, our friends drove us in an old jeep to the airport. The hood kept popping open and up so we had to stop to close it. Once we got to the airport, we found only the airport attendants present and no other passengers. We quickly went to the check-in station and were told the plane was already about to leave. Somehow our tickets showed the wrong time. Anne saw a door just over the baggage area that was open: 'Sally, let's go stop that plane!' She dashed through the door, and I ran after her, both of us with our suitcases. We saw the plane and waved it down. The pilot opened us cockpit window and said he was sorry, but once the engines had started, he could not let us on.

Of course, all the customs officials had run after us and they took us back into the building. We passed by the bar and a man at the bar stopped us and asked if we had a problem. We told him we had a workshop in Nairobi the next day, and needed to get back. He said he was flying a private 12-seat Lear jet back to Nairobi to pick up some passengers, and when he returned, we could fly with him to Nairobi if we could get permission to go with him. The officials took us to their small office, we told them our story and asked to see the supervisor. But they said the supervisor was on holiday. We asked where he lived. 'Oh, just down the road' was the answer. So we hopped into the jeep, drove to the supervisor's house and into his driveway which really was his lawn. When we stopped the car, the transmission of the jeep fell to the ground along with copious amounts of oil. Oh wow, what a start. Tanzanians are very gracious and welcoming, and the supervisor came out of his house, welcomed us inside and we told our story. He said, fine, of course, but could we give him a ride back to the airport. When we confessed our problem with the transmission, he laughed and offered to drive us in his car. Now we had the permission, we waited for the pilot to return.

Once we were in this wonderful jet, the pilot circled over Mount Kilimanjaro, and then low across the Serengeti nature reserve to see the wild animals. If you have seen the movie *Out of Africa*, we had that same glorious experience of seeing the animals from the air. When we arrived in Nairobi the pilot asked if we had a ride home and of course we did not, so he even drove us home.

Some of the lessons learnt from this experience: I learnt that often some government money is given basically in the government's own self-interest and not to benefit those in receipt of it. A personal reflection is that my immediate instinct at the airport counter was to follow Anne through the open door. This was a metaphor for much of our relationship. And a third point of learning was that small miracles can happen, such as our flight over part of the most beautiful land in the world. What a blessing.

Work was the center of our lives; however we would take time off to go to the Indian Ocean for one- week holidays, see movies, play tennis, and go out to dinner with friends. A tradition developed by which we went to Enda Byrne's family for most of Christmas Day, which was delightful. On the following day (Boxing Day), Enda, Anne and I would go to the annual famous horse racing event put on each year. When we got to the track, Enda would have spent the week before looking up the form of each of the jockeys, trainers and horses in the big race. I would immediately go to the betting stations to find out the odds for each horse. Anne would go to the horse ring to look at each of the horses, deciding on which horse looked the most handsome and would come back to us to say things like 'I love that chestnut horse so will bet on that one.' According to this system we would place our bets (probably about five dollars on our now favorite). My recall now is that none of us ever won.

After six years of intense work, we believed we now needed to consolidate the diocesan teams so they could extend bi-lateral aid to each other. We also thought that although DELTA was a strong program, a longer 6-week residential program would bring the work to a deeper level. This was called DELTA PLUS. We found outside resource people including a brilliant political economist, James Okraro, and others in fields of organizational development and spirituality.

In the middle of the course, a few participants stopped the process, demanding to know our team's budget and expenses and alleged that our team, and especially Anne and I were holding onto power. The central team had expanded, so we felt this was a false accusation. Anne was more devasted than I was. With a one-day break, I prepared our budget on newsprint, and showed that we were taking a monthly pay at the level of Kenyan secondary school teachers, which amounted to at that time about $3,500 annually. We opened up discussions about how to de-centralized work. The 'revolt' quieted down to a small murmur of two participants, and DELTA PLUS continued.

At the same time in Kenya a rumor of a national underground campaign with a document critical of the national government was being circulated to local activists. After DELTA PLUS, some of the local DELTA activists got copies of this document that was being circulated by one of the priests working in the DELTA program. One of the development coordinators was arrested by the local police and interrogated for a number of days. He was finally released, only to find one of his co-workers had turned him in to the police. This coordinator shrugged it off, but eventually that staff person was released from her post. Intrigue was now becoming very obvious in all parts of Kenya.

We continued with the DELTA and WINDOW phased training program as well as diocesan specialized workshops. In 1979, Anne and

I were invited by the International Grail to give a one-week course on adapting Freire to Grail work before an International Grail Assembly (IGA) to be held in Portugal. I had also been asked to help facilitate the IGA. I therefore flew to Portugal earlier in the year to plan the design for the IGA with the leadership team. We invited Thelma Awori and Jeremias Carvalho (a Portuguese priest who was working in Kenya and had partaken in the DELTA program) to come co-train with us. Over 40 Grail members attended. Ninety-seven members were a part of the Assembly.

Portugal had been ruled by a dictator, President Salazar and on April 25 1974, the military had overthrown his dictatorship in a non-violent coup. This was dubbed the 'Carnation Revolution' as ordinary citizens took to the streets, embraced the soldiers, and gave them carnations or put carnations into their rifles. The military group invited the President of the Grail, Maria deLourdes Pintasilgo to join their group. Maria described this time to Anne and me during her visit to us in Kenya and Tanzania. Maria said that the military officials were mainly focused on keeping the peace and issues of security within the State. They deferred the social issues mainly to Maria. Maria and Anne had been long term friends when they both had been in the Student Catholic Movement called Pax Romana. Their friendship lasted over many years.

Maria described this period as providing more democracy without a civilian government. How did this happen? Teachers, students and parents saw a vacuum in the school system and gathered together, school-by-school, and decided on the curriculum that would serve their families and kids best in the future. Bank tellers began to see that the very rich were starting to send their wealth to other countries, like Switzerland. Rather than waiting for a government policy to restrict these transfers, the bank tellers, themselves, just refused to move wealth out of Portugal. There were factories making colored television sets that the workers had no chance of purchasing. Workers in a number of factories decided to convert their factories to make products that their own communities needed. Democracy on many issues and levels began to thrive.

A few years later, the military government agreed to having an election. This was strongly supported by the United States who quietly backed one candidate. Maria deLourdes ran on an independent ticket and led in the polls for some time; however, money from outside sources overcame her bid to be Prime Minister. Coalition governments are common in some European countries as many parties vie for leadership. In 1979, no coalition government was formed and the President of Portugal appointed Maria as interim Prime Minister. This happened a few weeks before the International Grail Assembly was to take place in Portugal.

Maria decided to give her first public speech as interim Prime Minister at the International Grail Assembly. The morning before her arrival after lunch, a team of Portuguese government security agents came to this center to check out the place. After lunch, many of us 97 Grail members dressed in our national outfits and waited outside for Maria to arrive. We finally saw a trail of 5 cars driving up the mountainside road. Her limousine drove up to our group and the security detail jumped out of the car and looked quite perplexed as we were singing a welcome song at the top of our voices. Maria got out of the car, and none of us moved. Suddenly, Anne (who had known Maria for ages) moved forward and embraced Maria, and we all moved in to do the same. The confounded security police had no idea what to do.

Maria gave a one-hour speech of what she would do as the new Prime Minister. It was fantastic and our applause grew with each policy she put forth. Maria also mentioned that as the previous government was relinquishing power, they increased the salaries of all government workers, which would cause major deficits. So, her first act was to lower these salaries, which was quite painful for the government workers. At the end of her speech, a Grail member noted that these policies were wonderful, but Maria had not mentioned anything about military spending. We all had a great chuckle and left it at that.

During this International Grail Assembly, there was only one big room that served as the dining and meeting room. Before and after each meal, the chairs and tables had to be rearranged. There was a backstage crew headed by an American, April McConeghey, who said to me, 'Okay Sally, I will be furniture facilitator and you facilitate the people.' That was no easy task three times a day for eight days. Also, at this Assembly, an Indian Grail member had brought three other Indian women with whom she worked who were not Christian. We had scheduled a closing Catholic Mass and a few country representatives objected to the Indians taking communion. The Indian women were very hurt, and suddenly felt excluded. In solidarity, I also did not attend the closing mass and spent time in discussions with these women.

The strongest lesson was that it is better to 'err on the side of inclusion rather than exclusion'. Later I would also add to this that inclusion does not necessarily mean the use of money of a parent body who have fiduciary responsibility for funds. The other lesson I learned was that no matter how high up a person rises in terms of power, they are just as human as we are and thus can be welcomed or challenged, like a 'friend'.

Anne and I continued our work back in Kenya with the DELTA and WINDOW training programs and diocesan workshops, often having to split up because of demand. At one workshop, we had a heated discussion about the continued poverty in Kenya. I challenged quite directly a bishop who was present in this workshop and who downplayed this reality. Later that morning at teatime, I thought to myself, wow, that was inappropriate for me to be so outspoken in my role as a facilitator. I then thought, perhaps I am experiencing burnout. When I got back home to Anne in Nairobi, I told of this experience and shared my thoughts. I also suggested that as the team was doing so well, it might be time to leave. This was of course difficult for Anne, but some time later, she agreed.

Before we left for the IGA in Portugal, we had set up a small international DELTA phased program with participants from India, Liberia and Zambia. There were about ten international guests/participants with 25 Kenyans. We scaled this down to a six-week program, with international participants going with some Kenyans to their home places in-between residential one-week sessions. At the last session, we had a closing mass. This became a concern as not all of the International participants were Catholic. At an open meeting, tempers began to flare up, and one of our facilitators who was not Catholic intervened by saying, 'Well, who *owns* the mass anyway?' Of course, there were traditional responses, but it posed a question which we discussed for hours.

The Indians who attended this program in Kenya then invited Anne and me to give a six-week course on Freire and the participatory methods to a group of around twenty Jesuit priests, some nuns and a few lay people. This was held in 1980. We suggested we bring two Kenyans with us, which included a priest, Fr Macopiyo, and a trainer from Maasailand, Peter Kisopia. When we arrived at the Indian city then called Bombay, our Indian hosts drove us from the north to the south of the city, showing us the increased poverty – people first living in shacks, then under plastic roofs for sleeping areas, then a plastic mat to sleep on and then either sleeping on newspapers or with nothing under them. Bombay at that time had a population of about fifteen million people, one-third larger than the population of all of Kenya. Peter remarked he had seen more people on the streets of Bombay than lived in all of Kenya. He may have been right.

The venue was in a 'small' town of 150,000 people of Bharuch, near Ahmedabad. We found there were no locks on our cottage door and observed that those who drove here and there left their keys in the car ignition. The explanation was that this was a 'dry state' (meaning no alcohol sold anywhere) and so it was safe. We also saw women walking alone in the town at night with no fear.

During the workshop we found that Peter was completely silent. We could hardly get a word out of him. He was in total culture shock. We continued with the workshop with team meetings, including the Indian hosts. One night, I suddenly woke up to what sounded like Anne laughing and laughing. 'Are you okay?' I asked her. 'What is happening?' Anne replied that she had had dream where the team was trying to sort out how to get the whole group to be on the 'same page' in terms of culture, economic and political divides. So, Peter, in Anne's dream, suggested that we build a shrine to Our Lady's teeth as there were many shrines in India and one to 'Our Lady' was more Catholic. This caused Anne to laugh which in turn made me laugh as well. We never told Peter about this dream but we did smile about it once in a while during the course.

There were a couple of big points of learning for me during this time. The Indian team had arranged that we visit a textile mill. The one we went to had over 1,000 workers; the noise of the looms was ear shattering and the lint was everywhere in the air. The next morning Anne used a poem from Milton on the satanic mills for meditation. She quoted the entire poem by heart, as this was during the time when there was no internet. Part of that poem reads:

> And did the Countenance Divine,
> Shine forth upon our clouded hills?
> And was Jerusalem builded here,
> Among these dark Satanic Mills?'

I realized that many times I was trying to get Anne to help with some of the administration of the workshops we implemented in Kenya, I was trying to turn her into 'me' – while she was a poet through and through.

During the last week of this six-week workshop, I noticed that the caste system had never been addressed. Suddenly, a lay woman during another discussion said, 'We need to talk about the caste system here.' I responded by asking what specifically she meant. She replied, 'Well, I expect the caste system to disappear in the near future.' In my American approach I asked her when she saw this happening. Her response was, 'For sure in the next 250 years.' I was totally overwhelmed by this remark, as I could think in 3-5 year terms, let alone the Kenyans, who often thought in 3-5 month terms – as life at the survival level is geared to very short timelines. This really taught me a lesson on understanding time. India has a rich and very long history compared to so many countries in the world. Historical analysis is a vital component of critical consciousness.

Returning back to Kenya, we continued with workshops already scheduled in dioceses. But the time for our departure was growing closer. With the team and all of the main DELTA workers in the now eleven dioceses, we held a two-day farewell party. We planned this to be at the top of Ngong Hills, a fairly untamed park in the Maasai diocese and about ten miles from the center of Nairobi. The day before this party, a cold front settled in and the weather forecast suggested rain. We then decided we would have an afternoon party on top of Ngong Hills and then move to Enda's house and large veranda for a mass and a meal. At the party we reminisced of times together, sang songs, danced, Anne did masterful cartwheels with Enda's six-year-old daughter, while we huddled together to keep warm. The mass and dinner were splendid and the goodbyes sorrowful.

Reflecting on the United States' use of aid funds to countries of the South, I mentioned earlier about requesting 40 typewriters for the school I taught in, in Ethiopia. They sent only 20 typewriters as the company from which they purchased those typewriters would only sell them to our government with a metal table and chairs, which were not needed by us. In Kenya, we learned that US AID (United States Agency for International Development) had given a grant of $10 million to upgrade Kenyan television. Of this about $8 million was for new equipment that had to be produced in the USA, thus $8 million would stay in the USA. One million dollars would be for United States experts coming to Kenya, so that money stayed in American pockets. The final one million dollars went for scholarships for Kenyans to attend US colleges. That money also stayed in the USA.

A different lesson was how corporations operate in other countries. One of the pineapple canning corporations came to Kenya and asked the Kenyan government for the following in order to set up their factory in farmland near Nairobi. They asked that roads and electricity be available near the local small pineapple farmers so that they could bring their produce to the factory. They asked that they not pay taxes on their profits for several years. They also asked for an interest-free loan to build their factory. All these 'requests' were granted, assuming that the corporation would deliver on the 300 new jobs that would be created. A factory was built. Several years later the corporation came back to the government saying that they had a problem. The pineapples that these 100 small farmers brought to them were all of different sizes. Some were short, some tall, some wide, some thin.

They did not fit evenly into the machines. The corporation therefore would like to purchase all of the small farms and the farmers would get work in the factory. Permission granted. These 100 small farmers lost their land and ended up as factory workers. The exploitation of a country is a dramatic and horrendous story. My lesson here was that you have to fit into a 'machine' in order to have 'progress'.

Anne and I took two months to close off our work and pack up our possessions, selling and giving away most of what we had accumulated. We had arranged to have a sabbatical year at a USA Grail Center just north of New York City in a small town called Cornwall-on-Hudson. Anne had decided to travel via Brazil where she knew a Grail member who worked with the Base Christian Communities (which was a major inspiration of our work). I decided to travel via Portugal where I had become friends with Grail members there.

In Lisbon, I stayed with Isabel Allegro, a Grail friend from the 1979 IGA who had an apartment next door to Maria deLourdes and her close friend, Teresa Santa Clara Gomes. We ate meals together and probably solved all the problems of the world. Isabel invited me to a political meeting as Portugal was about to enter into a national election. I, of course, could not understand much of what was said. However, I kept hearing the phrase 'in principle' come up. I later remarked to Isabel on the way home, that perhaps the Portuguese use the term 'in principal', the British use the term 'in theory', and we Americans use the term 'in fact'. Of course, in the States when we use the term 'in fact', it may not really rely on 'the facts'. Perhaps it is a way to deter others from countering an argument?

Cornwall-on-the-Hudson, New York, Paris, and more separations

After Anne's travels to Brazil and mine to Portugal, we met at the Grail Center in Cornwall. The Grail members residing there had set up a program of meditation and quiet. It was called Metanoia. Anne would use her early morning hours in meditation, yoga, and reading serious books, a discipline she kept for the rest of her life. Anne also observed morning and evening prayers. I had set myself up for a study program on the political and economic conditions in the USA reading and summarizing heavy academic material. We also wrote articles together for the International Grail called 'Breaking Barriers and Building Bridges'.

Anne and I had been invited to Paris for an international program sponsored by INODEP (an ecumenical center studying Freire's methods and analysis). Sr Claudette Humbert, the director, and Fr Filip Fanchette had come to Kenya earlier after the DELTA PLUS experience and they were both most welcoming. Sr Claudette invited us to stay in the guest apartment and to have our meals with their sisters. The program itself had about thirty participants, of which two-thirds were from Latin America. They held separate discussions in Spanish while English-speakers worked with Filip.

During our English-speaking group discussions, each country's participants were asked to give a socio-economic-political analysis of their country. We had teams from India (population of about 800 million people), the Seychelles (population of 66,300 people), Kenya (population now grown to 16 million), and a few other countries.

We each had a half day for our presentations. Here is India with its huge population, a caste system, multiple languages and tribes that would take days to analyze. And then the Seychelles with a very small population and mainly one language and culture. When the team from the Seychelles presented their analysis, one man pulled out of his back pocket a piece of paper with the government's official statistics for their country. We could all read this at a glance and found there were more pigs in the Seychelles than people. We all had a good laugh about this, but ended up discussing their strategic geographic position in the world, which added to our broader understanding of geo-politics.

Being part of this INODEP experience enabled us to form some long-lasting friendships that became very important twenty years later. We also had wonderful times in Paris, which brought a lightness of heart.

We returned to Cornwall and dug into our quiet time, studies, and the more mundane tasks of running a retreat center. Every week when a group left after their event, we cleaned the big house, stripped the beds and did laundry, shoveled snow or mowed the lawns and planted flowers or vegetables. We also rotated cooking the main meals for the eight of us residing on the property. When my turn came, I always found something to cook that would take no more than thirty minutes to prepare. These domestic chores built our community with laughter that eased minor tensions (like how to fold a blanket properly), where we also laughed at ourselves.

The question of where Anne and I would plant ourselves in the future was always lingering. Four of Anne's nieces and her nephew lived in Zimbabwe. Anne's sister Joan with husband Jimmy, lived in Lesotho. Anne had a big pull to be with them, while I was ready to get down to work in the USA. Anne decided she would go to Zimbabwe and I found work with a community organizing project in Cincinnati, Ohio. Again, another farewell, though we both said this was temporary.

I had found a volunteer job in Cincinnati with a group called Citizen Action Alliance. Cincinnati had a number of chemical companies on the north side of the city who were polluting the water and air with toxins and not labeling toxins that the workers were handling. Citizen

Action Alliance was working on promoting a city ordinance to restrict these practices through a door-to-door campaign to support this Right-to-Know ordinance. I was able to find a room in the house of my former mentor's ex-wife, Petra Hawley. This arrangement worked for me.

About five months later, Anne called from Zimbabwe. She had been interviewing various leaders in the council of churches, the Catholic Bishop's Conference, a literacy organization, and the Jesuits' Training Center. The literacy organization said they would like to have training in implementing the Freire method of literacy work. On this call, Anne asked if I might be interested in working on this literacy campaign. I, of course, had been missing Anne very much, so I hopped on a plane and joined her.

Anne was staying with her nieces and nephew and I joined them. We immediately went house hunting and found a small 3-bedroom house near her family. Again, we went to auctions and found the basics for furnishing our new space. This house had an avocado tree that produced fruit in abundance, so we had a lot to give away.

I worked with the literacy organizations team and community leaders, helping to train literacy teachers and making sure they were up and running. Sr Janice from our Kenyan days was in Harare working with returned combatants from the liberation struggle. Zimbabwe had achieved its independence from white minority rule in 1980. The veterans group also asked us to give workshops. Anne was working with the churches and the Jesuit Training Center. Out of the blue, SWAPO, the South West Africa liberation movement, still in exile, asked us to develop a literacy project for those in camps scattered in numerous countries outside South West Africa. We said we would do it if they brought their potential trainers to Zimbabwe where we would do the training over a one-month period. This meant developing the posters and actual written materials for them to carry back to their camps.

Zimbabwe was experiencing a petrol crisis and petrol was rationed. Consequently, the team we had pulled together to work with SWAPO travelled to the training site each day in one car. I then stayed at the nearby petrol station, putting two cars in a long line to get petrol. It took at least 1-2 hours to get about five American dollars' worth of petrol. I would then take one of the cars out to the training site and work with the team. I assumed the responsibility of getting a printer to print the posters and other materials in the last two weeks of this program. We had a farewell celebration when all was completed. Many months later we heard that the leadership of SWAPO had refused to use our literacy program, as it had the potential to be critical of some of the camp regulations and practices. This was sad news.

During this time, a Zimbabwean publishing house, Mambo Press, approached us to have the training manuals we had produced earlier to be published. These old manuals were done on stencils in Kenya and no longer of use. Anne and I worked on an outline, read a number of African writers to add more context for African readers, and added African proverbs in the texts. The most difficult part was to decide on the first chapter. We debated about chapter one for days. Finally, we decided to write all of the other eleven chapters, as those were clear. We also knew the book would be very long, and practitioners would find it difficult to use in a workshop setting. So, we split this book into three parts: book 1 on adapting Freire's methods; book 2 on trust building in teams and communities, and book 3 on socio-economic analysis, organizational development and enabling organizations to use participatory management practices. We divided up the chapters to work on, with Anne editing my English. I would take the final copy of each chapter as it was completed and type the manuscript in triplicate on my old manual typewriter. After our proofreading, we were able to write the first chapter quite easily. When released, the books were called *Training for Transformation*.

These books were first published in 1984 and reprinted fourteen times. In 1995 we revised them and they have since been reprinted five times. In 1995 we also added book 4 to this collection. The fourth book addresses specific issues not covered in books 1, 2 and 3. It includes sections on ecology, gender, culture, racism, and governance. Mambo Press was located in Zimbabwe and in about 2005, the country ran out of major sources of ink for printing. We then found the E. F.

Schumacher Institute Press, now called Practical Action Publishing, in London, to publish and promote all the books.

At first they sold with only a slow increase in sales. Oddly, since 2010, more books have been sold than ever before. We were never sure why the surge in sales.

Another change of countries

I was 'brought into' Anne's family at this time. Several members of the family were going through a number of ups and downs, and like a 'good aunt', I had many discussions about their situations. At the same time, we gathered as family, and also Joan and Jimmy would come to a national camping site for holidays. However, I was starting to feel this country was too small. Every action or work undertaken was known to others, and I was feeling this wasn't the best place for me to be. I told Anne that I wanted to find work in the USA and would she please join me. Although she was in the middle of programs with a number of groups, I decided I would hunt for a job. Anne had been approached to teach part time at the Pacific School of Religion in California and I had heard of an opening with the YWCA in California. There was a Grail Center in San Jose, near San Francisco where I could stay. Off I went (again), with Anne most likely joining me in a few months' time.

I interviewed for the YWCA director's job and came in second. The reason they gave for my not getting the job was that while they loved my experience, it wasn't what they were looking for. I then searched in the Bay Area for other organizing jobs, coming in second again. I applied for an Amnesty International position in Boston where they flew me out for an interview, and about this time, a priest friend from Nairobi had found a job with a Returned Missionary Association for Anne in Washington DC. I went to Boston for the job interview. As I walked into the interview, I had this immediate hesitation that working with such major human rights abuses would be emotionally difficult for me. I did not do a very good interview and later heard I would not be getting the job. I felt relieved.

With Anne being offered the job in Washington DC, I left for Washington. Within days I had bought a car, and found a lovely house to rent half a block from Sligo Creek Park, which stretched for over five miles. I found a volunteer position with Project Vote!, an organization registering new people in disenfranchised communities to vote in a dozen states. In the meantime, Anne was travelling to the USA via Ireland where she was giving some workshops.

While she was there, Anne had a phone call telling her that her sister Joan and brother-in-law had been in a car accident and Joan had been killed instantly. Jimmy was in a coma. Anne called me and asked if I would find Alice, Joan and Jimmy's youngest daughter who was working with a church group in DC, and get her on a plane to be with her father. It was late in the afternoon but I was lucky enough to find someone in the office where Alice was a volunteer. I explained the situation and we met up to go to a bowling alley where Alice was with a group of teenagers. There, I told Alice of her mother's death. I had already organized an air ticket for her to fly to Lesotho and I took her to her apartment to pack. The next morning, once I had got Alice onto the plane I called Anne to tell her the arrival time.

Jimmy died just after Alice arrived. The funeral was held soon after, with the church packed for this beloved couple. Some suggested they should be made saints as a couple by the Catholic Church. Anne then continued to the USA to our new home. My mother gave us some money and we bought secondhand furniture so we got settled in, again.

I heard of a job as legislative director of Church Women United (CWU). This was an organization which was formed by progressive church women from 28 denominations in all 50 states. CWU had a policy that at least half of their Council needed to be women of color. During the interview for this job, I was asked what my career goals were. I replied by saying I didn't have any career goals other than dedicating my life to social justice and empowering women. When I got home that night I called my mother who was a member of CWU and really wanted me to get this solid job. I said I wasn't sure as I might not have responded well to their questions. The next day I got the call offering me the position. At last both Anne and I were in the same city and doing work that had meaning for us, albeit separately.

The lesson for me from this interview was - just to be myself.

My father (back row, second right) as a young man, with his family.

My parents on their wedding day.

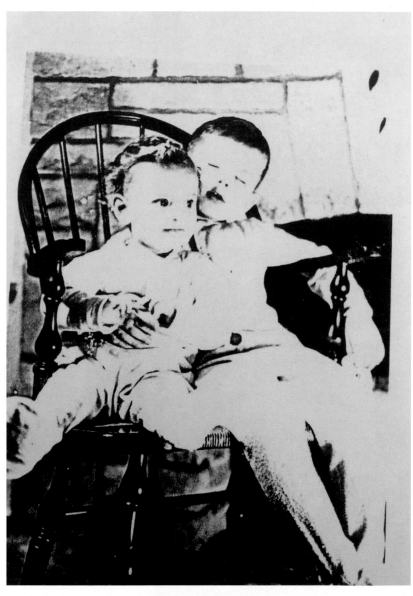

Me with my eyes wide open to the world
(and my brother Don, asleep).

Portraits of me aged 5 and aged 10.

Me as a 'helper' at an early age, and (in the middle) as a teenage cheerleader.

Alongside a fellow Ethiopian teacher while in the Peace Corps.

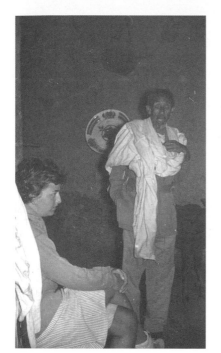

Images of me in Ethiopia (left, in a neighbour's house) and Kenya.

Anne Hope (top, and bottom in Kenya with me
and Enda Byrne).

In action as a lobbyist
on the White House
South Lawn, and with
a Fair Share team in
South Africa.

Training for Transformation; a photograph of the first group in 2002 and with director Ntombi Nyathi.

Anne at our home in Cape Town, and with me at the
Grail Centre in Kleinmond, South Africa.

The Washington years

As I reach this part of my story I find I have very mixed emotions. The work on Capitol Hill was stimulating, expansive, and drew on many of my talents. At the same time, my relationship with Anne was becoming more filled with tension, and I started drinking more every evening. Let me start with the work.

Washington DC is filled with lobbyists. The Pentagon could draw on all of its generals and experts to continue increasing military spending while funds for serious issues facing ordinary citizens were cut or eliminated. I had heard the Pentagon could draw on over 45,000 people to lobby. Corporations had thousands of lobbyists to protect their interests and tax breaks. The religious community had at most 30 or so people working on common issues. This certainly was a David and Goliath set-up.

The interreligious community worked together in different task forces: military spending and foreign policy, poverty, women's issues, civil rights, the environment and several others. A number of denominations had multiple staff so they could have different people focusing on discrete policies. CWU only had me. Within the year, I found funds in CWU to hire a second person in our office to work on domestic issues and I took on military spending, foreign affairs and civil rights. This worked very well with all of the staff from our separate religious groups sharing information and writing to our respective state and local groups. As one person said when I arrived, he could take leadership on two issues and would be a follower on others. We called each other often to get new information to keep our own networks up-to-date.

During the first weeks in the job, I decided to call all of the individual state CWU coordinators working on justice issues. I wanted to find out what their major concerns were so as to link them to legislation nationally. One morning I called a number that I thought was in Arkansas, in the south. I asked the woman who answered about civil rights in her state. And the woman said, I don't know if you know but you have called Alaska and it is only six in the morning! We had a great chuckle. I thought I knew 'my country' even though I had been 10 years in Kenya and then Zimbabwe. This was very humbling and made me a lot more careful about abbreviations of state names.

Over the eight years I was the legislative director for CWU, I focused my attention on budgets, blocking aid to the contras in Nicaragua, and South African sanctions. There are a number of ways to be a lobbyist: individually going to senators or representative offices; joining a coalition on an issue and so working with trade unions, women's groups, or anti-war groups, etc.; or setting up phone banks to activate the grassroots in key Congressional Districts or states to pressure support or opposition to certain bills. I chose the latter two. Working in coalitions meant keeping up with the latest information about a bill and taking on motivating the grassroots for action. These were the years that Ronald Reagan was president – a man who declared ketchup (tomato sauce) as a vegetable for school lunches and also made plans to build an outer space shield around the United States to stop missiles from landing on USA soil.

Because of my focus on military spending and foreign affairs, I joined a group that had originally been the anti-Vietnam War effort on Capitol Hill and was now called the Coalition for a New Military and Foreign Policy. They had a staff of about eight people. After a few years, I became the chair of their board. One effort that we implemented was TV ads on no aid going to the contras in Nicaragua. A small group of us worked with a Public Relations firm that made 30-second TV spots. We came up with the Red Cross on the screen that slowly started to drip blood. Then followed the statement of stop the deaths and vote against aid to the US-sponsored contras in Nicaragua. We called our activists in the areas where Congressional representatives were still not clear about their vote. The cost of these ads ranged from $30 in small cities to $500 in bigger metropolitan areas. Just as those groups started to air these ads, the Red Cross came to us and said we could not use their emblem – which was fair enough, but it was a great experiment.

I knew a lot about South Africa because of my relationship with Anne and I worked with the Washington Office on Africa. I remember meeting a senator who said they wanted to keep a constructive engagement with the Apartheid government and sanctions would hurt poor people. I, of course, argued that the sanctions mainly hurt the rich and corporations, and that the religious and broad-based civil society organizations were all advocating for sanctions. She was not swayed. As the vote in the House of Representatives was scheduled within days, our coalition was clear. We did not have the votes to pass sanctions. (We had called congressional offices to find out where each representative was on this vote.) On the day of the vote in the late afternoon, I had decided to go home. A colleague persuaded me to come watch the vote in the Capital itself. So, we waited and waited as each vote was cast, and lo and behold, we won by three votes.

I later learned that the collapse of the Apartheid government in the late 1980s was due to many factors: the collapse of the mining industry and their economy weakening quickly; the internal resistance to apartheid by civil organizations; trade unions having coalesced and becoming quite powerful; the sanctions pressure from the international community; and, probably most significantly, Nelson Mandela's willingness to negotiate a settlement.

My part-time co-worker, Doris Green, who was working on domestic policies resigned to take up a full-time job. I had heard there were internships where I could find a co-worker. I went to the Mennonite Volunteer program and they suggested a young graduate, Nancy Chupp. This was summertime. I called her at her home in Indiana for an interview. My first question to her was 'Which do you consider to be the most important issue facing women today, sexism, racism, or classism?' I wanted to understand her analysis of our society. She later said it took her by surprise and she felt she kind of stumbled through that, but I was more than satisfied. She sounded very cooperative and a 'thinker'. I hired her. When Nancy arrived, I gave her a short orientation to our CWU work, how we functioned together in the religious community through task forces, and our own CWU policies. I then suggested she go to a hearing happening at that moment on Capitol Hill. She later stated that I whizzed her right onto Capitol Hill and plunged her immediately into the work.

In 1990, Bill Clinton became president of the United States. He delegated health care reform to his wife, Hillary. Her planning process was not very open to civic and religious groups and her plan was not the single-payer option many groups supported. A co-worker gave me an important book by Daniel Yankelovitch called *Coming to Public Judgment*. I found Yankelovich's approach to change quite similar to that of Paulo Freire, but he added a step. After looking at alternative solutions, he called for discussion and then to commitment of trade-offs – which I thought were *ethical choices*. I worked with a team of Congressional staff members, ethicists, health care providers, and those of us in the religious community to develop the ethical trade-offs on the health care system. I felt I had just invented electricity! This goes back to my early childhood experience of seeing the movie about Thomas Edison and thinking of becoming an 'inventor'. I was inventing a new approach to understand public policy – ethical choices.

Church Women United Council had just voted health care as the biggest issue we should all work on for the next three years. I formulated a workshop design that we could implement in key states that would be critical on a vote in Congress. I took this to our national director in New York, and she agreed and suggested that Nancy become the overall legislative director in Washington DC and I focus on health care reform by rolling the workshop out to nine key states. I agreed. My co-workers in CWU in the New York office thought this was reformist and not progressive. I argued that it was a different way to implement Freire's work with the middle class. They argued that Freire's methods were with the oppressed – not the middle class. I also stated that the health care industry was the biggest industry in our whole country. Nancy and I then targeted fifteen states where the Congressional votes would be most strategic.

I worked from home developing a 'training of trainers' workshop. I called all fifteen CWU state justice chairs, and found nine states willing to do this work. Their task would be to recruit some thirty women who would then take this workshop to local churches and civic organizations in their communities.

There also was the question of getting funding for these workshops and my travel to these nine states. I had heard that the Robert Wood Johnson Foundation was funding health care reform projects. I wrote up a proposal and sent it in and with my usual follow up call to ensure they received our proposal. We waited.

CWU was having its Council meeting in Los Angeles. I called into our office and was told the director of Robert Wood Johnson Foundation had called and I should get back to him. From a hot and humid public payphone, I rang Dr Sandy, who grilled me for a fairly long period of time. I kept coming back to ethical choices. He was sold and said yes to our $250,000 grant on that call. I rushed into the meeting and announced our success. We now had all the resources we needed.

This work resulted in over 150,000 people attending these workshops on ethical choices on health care. We also had a follow up questionnaire to participants to find out how much impact the workshops had had with others beyond the workshops and found people became spokespersons in the issue, had radio talks, and thought more deeply about public policy. Unfortunately, and to be expected, the health care insurance companies pumped over $25 million in TV ads that showed a husband and wife talking in their kitchen about the fear of losing their doctor if any health reform bills passed Congress. Goliath won that day.

Nancy and I kept in contact while I travelled around the country. We hired a part-time person in New York to follow up on workshops results. Anne had by this time moved back to Cape Town. As I only worked for CWU three-fifths time, I travelled to be with Anne. Nancy and I developed a lifelong friendship from our numerous years of working together. She and her husband came to work in South Africa later, and stayed with us in Cape Town.

Washington DC – my personal life

As described above, work on Capitol Hill was consuming much of my attention. This felt like the place I was meant to be and I was developing friendships with those with whom I worked. Anne in the meantime, was first working with the Returned Missionary Association and was then asked to work with the Jesuit Center of Concern. At home, she would bring up her not feeling 'at home' in the USA, with the culture of consumerism, and the way some people on the staffs she worked with just operated differently than what she needed or expected. Anne pursued a second Masters Degree in pastoral counselling that seemed to capture her imagination.

I had rented a house for us up on a hill overlooking the neighborhood and near this wonderful 5-mile Sligo Creek Park. After two years, we calculated that buying a house would be much more economical for us. We liked this house, but the owner would not sell, so we went house hunting and found a small two-bedroom house that backed onto a park and decided to buy it. We wanted more space in the living room and this house had a big attic and basement. Two US Grail women who were builders lived in New Mexico and Ohio and we arranged they would come for a month to renovate our new home; we would also recruit friends in Washington DC to do some of the work. We contracted a local builder to put in two skylights in the attic and knock down the small living room wall for more space and light. With the help of our local friends, we scraped paint off walls, drilled holes in the attic beams for electrical wires to go through, and had moments of eating pizza and chatting. A lovely community-building exercise. Within a month, we were ready to move in. Again, we asked our friends to help us move our furniture and boxes the six blocks from our old house. We now had a common home.

We both went into therapy, but Anne's therapist died unexpectedly. She found a new therapist. In hindsight, we needed a therapist who understood 'exile'. This didn't come about. Anne fell into depression and was prescribed medication, which I didn't understand at all, at that time. She was in contact with her nieces and nephews in Zimbabwe, and went to visit them about every two years. Her niece Clare had been studying agriculture on animal husbandry. In 1985 Clare was to give birth to a child she had conceived with a Zimbabwean co-worker. Anne went to Zimbabwe to be at the birth of Themba, arriving just as he popped into this world.

In Washington D.C., Anne joined a group called SAS (Sisters Against Sexism), which became a support group for her. It was intellectually rigorous and held innovative rituals and liturgies. I attended some of these meetings and most of the rituals on high feast days. But we somehow were not connecting with each other on a meaningful and intimate level.

My alcoholism

While Anne was in Zimbabwe, I would go to a Grail friend's house nearby to watch movies. One night we watched *The Breakfast Club*. This is a story of four teenagers who are in some trouble at school and have to come in on Saturday mornings for detention. The teacher overseeing them on Saturdays would label them, using terms like jock, nerd, or super queen. I woke up in the middle of that night and said to myself, 'I am an alcoholic.' Of course, the next day I moved back into denial that I was an alcoholic, though I had wondered for years if that might be the case.

Anne was back in DC and her youngest niece, Alice, was graduating from Harvard Law School. We drove up to Boston and stayed with our friend, Nancy Richardson. There we met Alice's fiancé, Bert, and attended her graduation on the Harvard lawn. I did note that this was the first joint graduation held by Radcliffe, which had been an all-women's college, and Harvard. On the stage there were seven men and one woman. So much for equality. After the graduation I was going to proceed to a large CWU Council meeting, and Anne would go on to the Grail Center in New York. I was to pick her up after my CWU meeting. On the way to Wesley College for my meeting, Anne said that she and Nancy had agreed that my drinking was becoming a problem and that I might well be an alcoholic. I of course denied this, but then she said she would leave me if I didn't stop drinking immediately. I stayed at the meeting and Anne drove off.

I called Nancy to talk about this. Nancy said that alcoholism is a disease, like hepatitis and I needed to go into treatment. That night I went to my drinking buddies in CWU, had one drink and left. My immediate boss at CWU was Marge Tuite. Marge had been diagnosed with hepatitis and when she arrived at this CWU meeting, her color was yellow and she smelled of bile. For the following four days, I walked to the meetings and meals and repeated this mantra: 'I am an alcoholic, which is a disease like hepatitis.' I smiled later, that with all this Freire methodology in my bones, I found rote memory worked. I never had another alcoholic drink from that day forward. Marge Tuite died two weeks later. She had been misdiagnosed and died of pancreatic cancer. Her death was my life.

Upon returning to Washington with Anne, I went to Alcoholics Anonymous and Anne went to the support group for those living with a recovering alcoholic. It was very helpful to me to see that alcohol was a poison for me. Hearing the stories of other alcoholics where they lost their families, their children, their jobs, and sometimes had ended up in fairly serious car accidents, recalled to my memory two things. I remember driving at night in Cincinnati years earlier and missed seeing a stop light and I drove through it. Thank goodness there were no cars on the road, but I remembered I was drunk. I also remembered that movie, *The Breakfast Club*, after which I had brushed off my insight that I was an alcoholic yet my subconscious was aware and alert to my addiction. Anne had also learned that relationships after a period of sobriety with a partner can change and become difficult. I, on the other hand, felt that an enormous amount of creativity was being released in me.

At the end of this year, we had a visit from Steve Biko's second wife, Mamphela Ramphele and her two sons. They stayed with us for several days, which was wonderful. The boys and I tried to play baseball in the snow in the park behind our house. We organized other South African exiles to join us for a meeting with Mamphela and our house was packed. We had become friends with another woman in exile, Olive Chisana, who later became the Director General of the Health Care system in the new South Africa. During this meeting, a big debate emerged between Olive and Mamphela. Mamphela was arguing strongly that before the negotiations between the apartheid government and the African National Congress (ANC) took place, the ANC must make a commitment to gender equality on all levels, including appointments to government positions. Olive countered that this was secondary to a class analysis and would slow up the process of gaining political power.

They decided, finally, that they just disagreed. Years later I had a meeting with Olive Chisana in her government office, and I asked her, what was her greatest difficulty in working in government. Her very quick answer was that she was not taken seriously by the men she worked with. Diplomatically, I did not remind her of the discussion with Mamphela at our house.

The Grail in the meantime was going to hold an international meeting of nucleus members in Europe. Anne was planning on going, as she felt that at the very least these were her 'people' and she didn't think that the nucleus members would mind her attending. Unfortunately, several did mind - and they brought up the issue of our relationship. Anne was deeply hurt, and I was furious. I tried to argue with Anne that I believed she was one of the most faithful people I knew to the Gospels and the church. We both had started the Grail in Kenya and been carrying out the work of the Grail during all of our years in relationship. Anne didn't fully accept this and went to a meeting in New Jersey where a group then said she could no longer be a part of the nucleus. She came home even more depressed: she had lost her country, her family, and now, the Grail (her people). We continued to grow apart.

As I wrote earlier, I was very focused on my lobbying and organizing work. Washington DC is a hyped-up city, where a lot of adrenalin kicks in. I recall back in the 1970s when I was working in Cincinnati, a friend pointed out to me that I often would fall in love with someone I worked with. As Anne and I were no longer working together and because of her depression, in hindsight, I think now that it was almost inevitable that I would be strongly attracted to someone else.

Anne decided to go to her youngest niece Alice's wedding in Holland in the summer of 1989. While she was gone, I went on a holiday with a close friend to the beach. I 'fell in love' with this wonderful woman. I then hid this fact from Anne when she returned. For the next three or four months, I was living a double life. Finally, I told her about this other relationship and said I needed a two-year sabbatical away from our life together. Anne was devastated, and I moved to another house about 20 miles away. We still saw each other from time to time, but these months were fraught with sadness and tensions.

The woman with whom I had fallen in love then started looking around for other possible relationships with men, and finally she decided that our relationship had to end, as it was not fair to string me along. Anne in the meantime had been invited by the World Council of Churches to run a workshop in the Philippines. I found out when she would be returning and met her at the airport to drive her home. I told her my affair had ended. She was fairly cold about this news. We met numerous times after that, and she had by this time received an appointment on the faculty of the Adult Education Department at the University of Cape Town. She was leaving in August. It was now 1990, when all exiles could return. I was in the middle of a great deal of work on Capitol Hill and, as I only had a two-thirds-time job, said I would come visit her for four months, starting in December 1990.

How did Anne and I find each other again? We came back together in stages from the summer of 1990 to the fall of 1993. Some clarity was gained in 1993, to which I will return later. The 'knot' or issue between us was that I found myself being co-dependent with Anne. When I told a mutual friend that I had left Anne and felt I was co-dependent on her, our friend said that was true for sure. If she asked me how I was, my answer was, Anne has a migraine. My life was focused on how Anne was. I also felt I had been following Anne's vision and I didn't feel I had my own life. We had lived, loved, and worked together for 20 years by this time. I was now almost 50 years old, and I wanted to explore who *I* was. We worked separately in Washington DC and therefore had developed separate friends. I was excited and full of energy while Anne was depressed.

We each went to separate therapists and also to therapy together. It emerged that Anne had not felt integrated into United States culture. I understood that, but as it was my own culture, I somehow shrugged off her unease with it. As I have lived most of my life being very focused and task oriented, it wasn't until the death of Anne's niece, Clare, in 1993, that I saw the wider picture of my life. Maybe for some it takes a shocking jolt to see oneself and one's relationships more clearly.

Cape Town

When I arrived in Cape Town in December 1990, I think Anne was trying to woo me with the beauty of the Western Cape. That is not hard to do. She took me to Cape Point, the beaches, the top of Table Mountain and we drove to Knysna where her brother's family and mother lived. We had Christmas together there, and there were a few moments when Anne and her brother, Bill, would exchange very different perspectives on the South African situation. Bill had never left South Africa during the years that Anne worked with Steve Biko, and then lived in exile for 17 years. Bill would often respond to Anne's descriptions of the atrocities committed by the Apartheid government by saying they were exaggerated.

Anne had rented a house in a Muslim community in Cape Town. I stayed with her for three months. She was working at the Department of Adult Education at the University of Cape Town. I also went up to the university and became friends with a Muslim economist, Iraj Abedian. The United States had just started the first war with Iraq. Iraj and I held a panel discussion on this US aggression. In 1991, the United States under President George Bush was about to pursue a limited war in Iraq. The religious community had been briefed by a former CIA operative who told us that the US ambassador to Iraq had informed Saddam Hussein that their conflict on the border with Kuwait was heating up and if the Iraqi army went to the border, the USA would not intervene. Two months later, Iraq was at the border, and the USA did intervene against Iraq. I offered to raise funds to start a Budget Project through the economic department that would simplify the New South Africa's national budget to be used with grassroots groups around the country. He agreed, though it took until 1995 for this to come to fruition.

I would work with Iraj again in 1995 to develop a non-profit Institute called the Budget Project. I also met dozens of women that Anne had come to know. Things were feeling possible for me to come to South Africa; however, we hadn't sorted out our own relationship. It would take us four years to do so.

1993 – Clare's death

Each year, I would go to Cape Town to be with Anne. On 12 November 1993 I got a call from Anne while I was in Washington DC. Her niece Clare had been abducted and disappeared. She was going off to Durban on the east coast of South Africa to be with all of the family to try to find Clare. Days went by with no news. Newspaper articles, the Catholic Church staff, and many friends were in touch with the police during all of this time. Finally, on the day after Thanksgiving, I was with my mother in Wisconsin when I received a call from Anne that Clare's body had been found in the bush by a shepherd with three bullets through her head.

I immediately booked a flight to Durban, South Africa and was met by Anne. We went to a Grail house where Anne was staying with Clare's two children, Themba (then aged 8) and Puleng (18 months). We tried our best to comfort and help the kids to feel secure. Clare's funeral was at Marianhill, just outside Durban at a mission station, well known for its activism. The church was quite full. At the end of the mass, it was announced that the grave diggers had hit a fairly large rock so that refreshments would be served while waiting for the grave to be dug. Anne and I then went and sat by Clare's casket in quiet meditation for over an hour. It was then I realized that these were my people, my family. I shared this with Anne a few days later and said I would move to Cape Town indefinitely. We were both strong women in different ways. We might have needed this separation in order to find each other again, differently, but with deeper roots.

In October 2019, Clare's son, Themba along with his cousins, Benjamin and his 7-year-old son Damian came to visit me at Pilgrim

Place. One cool evening, sitting on my porch, we started talking about assassination of Clare, Themba's mother. We had not taken in that this would have been Clare's 60th birthday, had she lived. In looking at our turning points and especially the grief we still held, we found how deeply wounded we all still were.

Although I was now committed to living in Cape Town and being with Anne indefinitely, I was still in the middle of the health care project in the USA. Anne was now working with a team at the University of the Western Cape that was focused on development education.

We started hunting for a new house. We both enjoyed looking at houses so we scoured the newspapers and made contact with estate agencies. We probably looked at more than 30 houses, all near the ocean but not too far away from the city center. The day before I was to go back to the USA, we were at a house I found suitable, but it had no ocean views. The real estate agent at that house asked us what we were looking for. We said something with a view. He said I have the perfect house but it is not open until tomorrow morning (the day I was leaving for the States). Next morning, we went to this house, which was not two blocks from Anne's old house. Anne walked up the 56 steps up to the house and I took the very steep driveway. It was a charming house with a veranda overlooking the back of Table Mountain, a slice of the Indian Ocean and across much of Cape Town. Anne loved it. I was thinking how great it was, but I said instead, 'Let's call each other upon my arrival back in the States.'

We did call each other and we said yes. The owners did not want to move out until October, which was fine, as I was only coming to live indefinitely the following January. We bought the house. A few months later Anne got worried about driving up this steep driveway. When she knew the owners would be at work, she went and practised driving up the driveway - and she made it. We now had a home.

GAP (Gender Advocacy Project)

During the times I was in Cape Town, I had met some women Anne had grown to know well. I interviewed a number of these women from the former underground African National Congress (the ANC), churches and women's groups. I asked whether it would be helpful to visit both Washington DC and Zimbabwe to compare ways in which women could have more influence on what would be the new government of South Africa after the elections in 1994. I found funding from UNIFEM, the women's part of the UN where our former colleague in Kenya was now the deputy director. While Anne and I were in Zimbabwe, the government had established a Department of Women's Affairs to enable women to have their voices heard. While in the USA, there were dozens of women's groups outside of government structures that advocated for women's rights. One issue posed at this time of transition in South Africa was how women's rights could most effectively be promoted, inside or outside government. It was also an assumption that the GAP between men and women was in terms of power, laws, and access to money.

The funding came through. There were enough funds to have six women come to Washington D.C. and then continue to Zimbabwe. I recruited two African women, two 'colored' (as was the term used then) women and two white women. I contacted a team in Zimbabwe to give these six women a one-week program to learn how the government's Women's Affairs Department was promoting women's rights. Upon my return to Washington DC, I found four organizations where the South Africans could intern for 3 weeks.

During the time this group was in the USA, we would have meetings every three days to reflect on their learnings about advocacy. These six women had known each other through some common work against apartheid in Cape Town, but they had not travelled, worked, or studied together. A few times, racism had reared its head between them and I had to intervene, to calm the waters.

While the team was in Zimbabwe, they had a field trip to women's groups in more rural areas. They found that peasant women felt quite alienated from urbanized women who had had more schooling.

When I returned to Cape Town on my next annual visit, the GAP group met together to share their findings. They found that the GAP was between women. The focus of their work in South Africa needed to be to bridge the gaps between women and bring forth the concerns of women from the grassroots up to the legislature. During an open workshop with over forty women present, GAP, as a separate organization, was formed. I was asked to be on the board.

A few months before the first democratic elections, the GAP staff had decided to press the ANC, the ruling party, to ensure that 30 per cent of all parliamentary seats and the cabinet be held by women. During one of the board meetings, I remember emphatically saying that as women were 51 per cent of the population, and so we should be advocating for 51 per cent of all positions to be held by women. I won the day. To our amazement, the ANC agreed to this position. Not all parties followed suit, but it was a big win for women. To this day, the ANC continues to have 50 per cent women in their Parliamentary seats and in cabinet.

Cape Town indefinitely

I described earlier how I had wanted to be an inventor during my early years. The next twenty years in South Africa was where this desire came to fruition - as a social inventor focused on critical consciousness, creating interventions that had strong emotional links with communities, and engendering participatory methods.

Prior to 1995, I had been asked by some funding agencies if I would facilitate a meeting of European Catholic agencies to discuss how to move ahead after the genocide in Rwanda. I had no experience with this country, nor had I studied about genocide, but I knew of resource people who could help with this process. I contacted Bethel Kiplagat who had been the Kenyan Minister of Foreign Affairs to ask him to be a resource person at this workshop. Others I recruited were Thelma Awori, now with the UN, and Enda Byrne, who knew these funders well. Each agency also brought special experts. Although the workshop did not produce a common strategy amongst the fund agencies, it did evoke new insights. For example, Rwanda was land-starved. Families had been torn apart because there was not enough land for all the sons to farm. Neighbors were angry with their neighbors because of land issues. Another insight was from a psychiatrist who had worked with holocaust survivors. He explained that each one of us has within us the ability to commit genocide. However, our cultures, religious beliefs, families have put layers and layers of prohibition on these attitudes/behaviors. In Rwanda, these attitudes and behaviors had been peeled away and allowed such brutality and massacres to occur. There was a huge silence after this presentation, and we took some quiet time to absorb it, for ourselves.

In January 1995, I finally arrived in Cape Town and of course was met by Anne with open arms. We settled into our new house with its amazing views of Table Mountain, the Indian Ocean, and much of the city of Cape Town. The house was all on one level, but I immediately tried to find a builder to add two rooms and a bathroom upstairs. Anne, as always, threw a big party for my arrival with friends she had made over these five years.

Local elections in South Africa

The national election took place in 1994 with the African National Congress (ANC), led by Nelson Mandela, securing 12,237,655 votes – 62.65% of the national vote tally. This victory earned the party 252 seats in the National Assembly and would go on to signify its future political dominance. Local (or municipal) elections were to take place in 1995. These elections were run by wards or smaller geographic sections.

Over the five years that Anne had been both working at the university and starting a women's training program, she had come to know a breadth of women activists throughout Cape Town. A number of these women were now in the National Assembly or cabinet ministers. We decided we needed to get to know our local area better so we started to attend ANC local meetings. We found some of these rather boring, but a working group was formed and a meeting held to decide on a candidate for our local area to run as the ANC candidate. An obvious split occurred between those who had been actively anti-apartheid in their area and those who had been in exile. We had become friends with a woman, Diane Salters, who had been in exile in the UK and had been a local government councilor for the Green Party. She had great experience that would be very helpful in our Cape Town Council. Of course, Anne and I supported her. During this rather fractured meeting, Diane was finally selected as the ANC candidate for our ward.

As I had had experience running election campaigns in the USA, I worked alongside Diane and a team to develop a strategy. This included door-to-door visits, telephoning, raising money, and securing an office on a corner of the main town in this ward, at a stop light. I, of course, always did fundraising. A number of former Nationalist political party members (the Nationalist party was often shortened to 'Nats' - read that term whatever way you wish) shifted to the ANC. Diane has reminded me that at one of our many fundraising events, one of the Nat members said to her: 'Keep that woman away from me – every time she comes near me she gets money out of me.' No need to say who 'that woman' was!

We also raised funds through a raffle of items donated by businesses. I bought a number of tickets in Anne's name as her name is shorter than mine, but did this unbeknownst to Anne. At the final thank you-celebration party, Diane drew the names of the winners of raffle items. The 3rd place winner was Anne Hope with a bottle of wine. Anne was surprised and accepted graciously. Finally, the first-place draw for a weekend at a beautiful resort on the Atlantic Ocean called Monkey Valley, just 20 minutes from our house. Again, Anne won. She gave back her bottle of wine, and we duly took our weekend at Monkey Valley. We later purchased a week timeshare during low season for us and for Anne's family to visit.

Fair Share

I had become convinced over the five years since coming to South Africa that political apartheid had been mostly abolished. This meant all South Africans, regardless of race, could reside anywhere, use any facility, and were 'integrated' into places where they had been banned. However, now South Africa faced economic apartheid. It was all well and good that you could go to any hotel and get a room or a meal, or ride the train in first class, but wealth was enormously divided against people of color. As I researched this I found out that of all countries in the world, the economic gap between rich and poor in South Africa was the highest. This gap has actually become larger from 1995 to 2019.

I had found funding for a Budget Project with Iraj Abedian at the University of Cape Town economics department. As we had enough funds, Iraj hired a woman to be an administrator and I hired Samkele Mhlanga, to work with me doing grassroots workshops. After some time, I realized three things: Iraj had disappeared for a trip to Washington DC but he would not tell me the purpose of the visit. Later I was to learn he was a consultant to the World Bank to work out an economic policy for South Africa called GEAR (Growth, Employment and Redistribution). However, this policy had nothing to do with 'redistribution'. It was focused on growth, which really means the economy is geared towards corporations and the rich. Secondly, he was not very interested in our grassroots work, but spent time with one or two other large organizations to press Parliament and the Cabinet towards World Bank policies. The straw that broke my back was that he was using the administrator for the Budget Project, thus project funds, for his personal assistant to book his flights and to type his documents for the World Bank. To me this was unethical, so I began searching for another avenue to do budget work.

Anne was working with a team at the University of the Western Cape. This university had been where liberation comrades had studied, so it had a progressive reputation. The team Anne worked with was called SADEP, the South African Development Education Program. Its director, Vivienne Taylor, along with her husband Allan, had been in exile, and she was a strong force within the ANC nationally. I had met Vivienne often so asked her if this budget work could be housed within SADEP. She agreed quickly. In several months, I hunted for more and new funding to expand our team. We would also find an office closer to where our team lived as UWC was quite far away from the center of town.

Samkele and I had been doing budget workshops, and found two other people who were very interested in expanding this work. We needed someone to do research on the national budget itself, as well as someone connected to grassroots activists. We also found a temporary home in the offices of DELTA (the women's training program that Anne had initiated). At one of our one-day planning meetings, we realized that calling this new organization the 'Budget Project' didn't say what we were about and we needed a new name. We went into a brainstorming session looking at our aims. One person said, 'we want a fair deal'. We liked that but then we said, no, we want our 'Fair Share'. Perfect.

As the work grew, and the building where we were housed was being sold, we found a space where the owner was willing to renovate the factory space into offices. At this time, European funders were still very interested in assisting non-profit organizations in this transition for South Africa. Our staff grew to seven members.

We developed a simulation game that took about 15+ departments of government that most affected people at the base. These included housing, health care, water, education, transportation, and others. We also needed to examine the tax structure, as any budget has income and expenses. A simulation is taking a slice of 'reality' and putting the picture of the larger issues into an experiential learning situation.

I will describe this 'budget game' here for those readers who are interested in this process. In a group of 30-40 people, the participants would be asked to form groups of 3-4 to name the major 2 issues that most affected their lives. These were collected in the whole group. We then put on the wall a piece of paper with a column for each of these issues and asked people to go to the one issue they wanted to discuss in greater depth, with no more than 5 people in each small group. These small groups were now proclaimed as the government Ministry of Education, Water, etc. Each group received a one-page information sheet about this issue, reflecting actual, real data which had previously been collected through our research. For example, with housing, the data showed the actual number of houses needed throughout South Africa at this time, the cost of self-built housing, the cost of commercially built housing, the present policy of government regarding building subsidized housing, the actual line item for housing in the national budget (which of course was a huge shortfall), and then the task of this small group. The task was to decide how they would best meet the needs of full subsidized housing for all in the country.

These discussions took a long time. The facilitator (who said she was the Minister of Finance), after about 45 minutes, would announce to the whole group that the government had not been able to collect enough money from taxes to pay for everything, so they had to either cut their own budget request, or cut another ministry. Each group was given another printed list of other departments and their budget for that year. The facilitator would also announce there would be a cabinet meeting (in a fishbowl in the center of the room) in say 30 minutes to discuss what each ministry needed and why, and where the cuts of the national budget would take place. Each small group could send one person as their Minister to the cabinet meeting. The others would be observers. These discussions often produced some 'out of the box', but humorous ideas!

This session lasted a whole morning. The afternoon session looked at taxes.

The 'real' work behind these workshops was gathering the data for each of the one-page sheets for each issue, all of the government departments, and taxes each year. The researcher and I would split up the issues and over a 2-3-month period, would have gathered all the information, usually starting in January and ready by a few weeks after the budget was released to Parliament and the public. This meant having a solid contact in each department.

The Finance Committee of Parliament would hold public meetings on the budget each year. I would attend these meetings. During the first year in developing this Budget Simulation Game, at the end of the first session of this public hearing, the chair asked if the public had any questions. I, of course, raised my hand and was called on to speak. I said to these Parliamentarians, the Minister of Finance and the head of the Revenue Service, 'I do not understand why you are thinking of cutting the taxes on the very wealthy in this country down to 30 per cent of their income and wealth. I come from the United States, and I have paid 35 per cent in federal taxes, 10 per cent in state income tax, and 5 per cent on local income tax. That means a total of 50 per cent tax, which I do not mind paying for my services. But you all are getting away with murder.' The chair immediately called for a tea break. When I went to also get some tea, the director of the Revenue Service came up to me and thanked me profusely for my statement. He said, he could not say this himself but it was extremely helpful. I then shared with him what we were doing with our budget workshops at the grassroots level and asked him if there was someone in his department who would help us every year to get the correct numbers on the seven different kinds of taxes that government collected. Without a blink, he said yes and gave me his card to call him in two days. I did and was set up for years to be given this information.

Another big piece of work we did at Fair Share was to hold a press conference the day after the national budget was released to Parliament. One of our staff would pull together four top economists, the heads of the Council of Churches, the trade union alliance (COSATU), and the national NGO Coalition. We would meet an hour after the national budget was presented taking some time to read and review the areas of our competence. The economists would share their broader view of the budget, then the rest of us would share areas of changes and shifts of priorities (those budget items like more money for housing versus tax cuts or military spending). These meetings would take 4-5 hours with food brought in through the evening hours. The next morning the heads of the national organizations would hold their press conference. These organizations would present an Alternative 'People's' Budget. Following the press conference, we would hold a workshop for more members of these national staffs to learning about the new budget.

As we rolled out these local workshops with community organizations, we realized that these groups did not seem to have the leverage with their local governments. As Fair Share was linked to a university and we were doing this work just a few years after local elections, local governments were also searching for a way to link with grassroots communities. Because of the history of apartheid, local governments did not have much credibility especially with black communities. In areas where we worked, we approached the local mayor and city manager and offered a 2-3 day workshop in their town. The format was 10 elected officials, 10 top administrators, 10 businesspeople and 30 community leaders. They went through a process (in mixed groups) of looking at the major issues facing their town, developing a mission statement together, their roles in reaching the goals of that mission statement, and identifying follow-up actions that each group would take. At the end of one of these workshops, a former apartheid government elected official came to me to say, this is what we all needed to break out of our own biases and party affiliation. This work continues.

During this time, with our economist friends and the national organizations of trade unions (COSATU), the Council of Churches and national non-profit organizations, we continued to analyze the national economy. As a collective, we asked for a meeting with the Minister of Finance (Trevor Manuel), at the Anglican bishop's house. This house had rooms for Bishop's Tutu's offices. At this meeting, we asked specifically about the Civil Servants' pension fund, which was huge. We argued that this fund could be used in part for infrastructure development of housing, health care, roads, etc. We did not think that the government pension fund needed to be treated the same as a private pension fund. A private pension fund needs to have enough funds (capital) to pay all pensioners at one time if that fund suddenly went bankrupt. Trevor Manuel's reply was that his team had just been in Russia, and that country was almost bankrupt – and he laughed heartily. I responded that it seemed to us that South Africa would not go bankrupt if it continued to grow the budget through taxes. So, I asked, 'Trevor, are you saying you expect the South African government to go bankrupt?' He made no reply to that point and we came to an impasse.

I did this work for four years. In 1999 the Grail group had decided to purchase the Grail Centre in Kleinmond (an hour east of Cape Town) and start the Community Development program in the surrounding district marginalized communities. I couldn't do all of this so found someone to take up the role of director of Fair Share. I had set up an advisory committee for Fair Share and one member was the head of the government department at the University of the Western Cape. Fair Share continues to this day as an Institute of the School of Government at UWC working with local civic organizations to advocate for basic rights and services in partnerships with local governments.

Finding the Grail Center

In about 1993, the former Prime Minister of Portugal, Maria deLourdes Pintasilgo, came to Cape Town for a meeting of former heads of State. As discussed earlier, Maria was a dear friend of Anne's from their student days in Pax Romana. Maria invited us to a cocktail party with these heads of State. It was a rather awesome affair, and I spotted former USA Defense Secretary, Robert McNamara in the crowd and went to talk to him. I told him I had been in the Peace Corps, and his response was he surely wished he had headed up the Peace Corps rather than trying to sort out the war in Vietnam. He also said that his son had joined the Peace Corps. Well worth the exchange.

A day later, Anne gathered together about 30 women from Cape Town to meet with Maria in our house. After the guests were gone, Maria said to Anne, you must start a Grail group here. True to her calling, Anne did. From 1993 onwards, about ten women would meet in each other's houses for a potluck supper, discussion of readings and meditation. Anne intuitively knew that starting a Grail group here had to have a majority of women of color. Anne and I, along with one other white woman, initially were the only white women in this Grail group. In 1998, we suggested that we needed a common file cabinet to keep all of our Grail papers from other countries and the International Grail. This idea grew into needing a small office; then a guesthouse so we could have a common space that could host guests.

We heard of a group interested in ecological education who had a property on the edge of Cape Town near an informal settlement. They were looking for partners. About five of us Grail members went to those meetings. After about a year with no clear path forward, we asked for the owners of the property to write up their goals and mission and hopes for the space. When they started this meeting with us, the presenter stated that the key was to have 'the right people' living at this Center. I brazenly asked, 'Who are the "right people", as for us as Grail, we would see those living on the property reflecting the demographics of South Africa.' A male owner of the property said that black South Africans were too busy making money or looking for lucrative jobs now that apartheid had ended. We Grail folks looked at each other. After a while we left the meeting and went to our cars. When we got about two blocks away, I stopped our car, flagged down the other Grail members. At the roadside we said to each other, 'No way'. Everyone was furious. Thus ended that saga.

Two of our Grail members at this stage, Nabs Wessels, who had worked for the Council of Churches and with Anne on the women's DELTA training group in Cape Town, and Samkele Mhlanga, who had worked with a literacy campaign organization and then with me in Fair Share, had said they would be willing to move to a conference center with their families to be community development staff. The four of us then went in search for a center. We visited several places. One place had been converted into a lovely retreat center and the owner came to greet us. We asked him why he was selling. In a very gravelly voice he said that the neighboring farms used a lot of fertilizer which had ruined his lungs. Well, that was a clear no for us.

A number of us Grail folks had gone to a town on the coast called Kleinmond. A colleague of Anne's, Ina Conradie, had a family home there. So Anne suggested we drive out there and we got in touch with a Real Estate agent in the town. The agent showed us a few places and then asked what we were looking for. We said something like a retreat house or place where 10-20 of us could gather. He said, I have got just the place for you and he drove us to a small resort called Brightwood Cottages, snuggled under the mountains. It was a cloudy, gloomy day. We went into the property that had about 26 buildings on it, of which twenty-two were 1, 2, or 3 bedroomed cottages. We said to the estate agent that this may be too much. That weekend was a Grail meeting so we described Brightwood Cottages. Everyone was keen to see it, so we arranged for the next weekend to rent a cottage for the afternoon.

We drove the spectacular coastal road in bright sunny blue skies and arrived to perfect weather. The place looked so much more appealing. Within an hour, the Grail group felt, 'this was it!'. As we were getting ready to go, a handsome, cheerful man popped his head into our meeting to ask if there was anything we needed. This was Joe Snyman. More than half our group knew him as a manager of a previous conference center with his wife, Heather. The group asked me if I could find the funds. I said that is what I would do - and I did. However, before we assumed ownership, I had asked Joe whether the center had broken even financially during the winter months. He said no. So, we delayed our purchase and occupancy until 1 September.

While we were waiting for all the paperwork to go through and funds to arrive, two Grail women from Holland came to visit Anne and me. Anne took them to see what we were hoping to purchase for a Grail Center and they were very enthusiastic. On their way back to Cape Town and stopping to overlook the Indian Ocean, they saw a rainbow and said, this really means it is meant to be. They later found some funds to help support our purchase of the Center. Anne and I sometimes hummed that song, 'Somewhere over the Rainbow'.

On Christmas Day 1998, Anne and I had been invited to Christmas lunch with new friends, the Templetons. They lived in community with about 8-10 other families or priests. I was still searching for funds to purchase the center. Peter Templeton was a great fund raiser and had been director of Catholic Welfare and Development in Cape Town where Anne had an office. So as Christmas dinner progressed to dessert, I asked him if he knew of any funders I could approach. He said nothing about funders, but recommended we bury a sacred medal, in good Catholic tradition. Someone had such a medal nearby and a Jesuit priest blessed it on the spot.

A friend from the USA, Nancy Richardson, then came to visit us. We knew her from the YWCA and then in Boston. We had this blessed medal, and when we took Nancy to see the Center, and as she was an ordained minister, we buried that medal under a large tree, with

Nancy, Anne and I blessing the center before we purchased it. Nancy then said, buy this now, don't wait. By the beginning of 1999, we had purchased the Grail Center at Kleinmond.

We all were panicked that we would not make enough money on a monthly basis to pay staff, maintenance and the like. Most of us Grail members knew many non-profits and faith groups in and around Cape Town. So, we all took the initiative to get groups to rent our new Grail Center in Kleinmond. We had raised enough money to convert one house into a dining room/kitchen, build a meeting room next door, and add public toilets. But the construction took until November. We used a living room in one of the bigger houses as the conference space. We took in more money during those first four months than we ever did again.

We took ownership of the Center in September 1999 and hosted a blessing of the property with more than 100 people for lunch held outdoors. Autumn weather can be tricky in this area, and on the day before the blessing, a huge wind and rainstorm descended. Staff and friends kept working away and by the morning of the launch, September 6, the skies were clear and we were ready. We served lunch for all, then we went from house to house, area by area, and blessed each corner of this Grail Center.

A Blessing

In the beginning, 15 billion years ago, time and space were born.
The universe flashed into a hundred billion clouds,
Out of which galaxies constellated.
In the spiral galaxies the flames of this beginning transformed
Into a new mixture of elemental potential.

These creative actions are not found in any other place in the universe,
So that the vanguard of creativity is contained in spiral galaxies
Where it is alone possible for new stars to be born.

Four and a half, distant billion years ago,
One particular spiral, the Milky Way, our own home galaxy,

Gave birth to a particular star, our Sun,
Whose own explosive birth formed in turn a gaseous disk
Out of which our solar system emerged.
This disk evolved nine planets.
The third from the sun,
Being at just the right distance and just the right temperature
To develop life, became 'the little blue pearl'
That we call Earth, our Mother.

Now we stand, conscious creatures, born of stardust,
Not just on Mother Earth, not just in Africa,
Not even just in Kleinmond,
But at this particular pregnant moment in time and
on this particular small and precious piece of earth
that has been entrusted to the care of the Grail,
in a graceful marriage of mutual benefit, to have and to hold;
to give and to receive the breath of life;
to protect and to enhance;
to marvel at the sound of the sea
and to whisper to the wind in the trees.

As we stand here
Enthralled at the sheer beauty of creation,
May our eyes be opened
To see that the blessing we ask is the blessing already given;
A place in the Divine Being in whom we live and move and have our
own small being;
A place of nature and in nature that brings refreshment to soul and
body;
A place of co-creativity
Raising Nature (and our own natures)
To places yet unknown and only partly glimpsed;
A place where searching unfolds
Into the discovery of the Holy Grail.

Catherine Collins, 1999

AIDS response

In this period, 1999-2000, the President of South Africa, Thabo Mbeki, made public that he did not believe that HIV was connected to the pandemic of AIDS. The Grail board that had purchased the Grail Center agreed that one of the programs at our Center would need to address HIV/AIDS. One of the program staff, Samkele Mhlanga, took this task on. Samkele began by calling all of the AIDS providers in Cape Town and the surrounding areas. She asked them about the gaps in responding to the AIDS pandemic. After contacting more than 30 agencies, she found that caring for the caregivers was a key component that was not being addressed.

Through our Fair Share connections, Samkele contacted Diane Salters, a psychotherapist, to see if she would work with Samkele, as a team, to roll out 2-3-day workshops with caregivers at the Grail Center in Kleinmond. Through this program they would reach 25-30 caregivers in each workshop. The objectives were to give the caregivers and counsellors (initially women, and later men, too) a rest and respite from their very challenging work, time to reflect on their own health, encourage awareness of their own needs, plus a 'tool kit' to help them deal with communication with their patients and the families and take care of themselves too. This tool kit drew mainly upon the basics of transactional analysis but also included physical exercises and breathing. It was seen as an important way of giving caregivers lasting tools for self-care that they could take home with them, real learning, and not just a one-off good experience. This program was participatory in its methodology and fostered group cohesion and a climate of transformational learning.

Within a few years, the pandemic had grown in South Africa; Thabo Mbeki had become more entrenched in resisting drugs to lessen the effects of HIV, and civil society had begun major protests led by the Treatment Action Campaign (TAC). Along with the director of the DELTA Women's Training Program, Mizana Matiwana, we believed that along with the Care for Caregivers program, there needed to be an advocacy program as well. By chance, a major funder of DELTA and the Grail programs was in Cape Town for a meeting of their recipients of grants. The program officer stated that HIV/AIDS was a critical issue for their agency. During a break, Mizana and I asked the program officer for a meeting. We shared with him the concept of our AIDS Response and the need to grow this program. On the spot, the program officer said yes to funding this expanded work.

AIDS Response moved their offices to Cape Town, hired five new staff members, and continued the Care for Caregivers workshop at the Grail Center. AIDS Response then built allies to work together on advocacy as well as wellness clinics in marginalized areas.

The work in surrounding communities

The Grail board that had now been set up for the Grail Center had stated that the Center was mainly for workshops with those marginalized in South Africa as the legacy of apartheid had continued. Two Grail members, Samkele Mhlanga and Nabs Wessels, agreed to move to the Center. Two of the houses were renovated with a house between their houses to be used as their offices. As I quipped at the time, they certainly saved transport costs to get to work!

Their main work would be community development in the three surrounding districts. They both travelled to these small towns to the township areas to pull together community leaders. The plan was then to have community leaders from say, 5-7 towns come together at the Grail Center for weekends to share their common concerns and enable them to gain some participatory leadership skills to expand their impact. These weekend training programs took place for a few years; however, after some time, fewer participants came to these weekends. The reasons given by many was they felt they could not leave their homes for fear of robberies or harm to their children. Adjustments had to be made for the work.

In response to such concerns, our staff then began one-day workshops in the townships themselves. Doing so proved quite fruitful as the communities gained strength to advocate for the issues most prevalent for them. Two of the major generative themes (themes that give life) were jobs and housing. None of us had had experience in these fields. Samkele knew of an architect-turned-community-housing-expert who lived in Cape Town, Joel Bolnick, who had started a project for subsidized houses in the townships there. We met with him numerous times to learn about some of the best practices that could be implemented in Kleinmond.

There was a large plot of land behind one of the primary schools in Kleinmond. This plot was on a very steep hillside, but had a wonderful view of the ocean. It was owned by the Department of Education. This land was also behind the so-called 'colored' area of town and near the township where over 4,000 Africans lived mainly in shacks. Samkele and Nabs then organized the local communities to advocate for subsidized housing on the land. In 2004, they held a protest march through the town to the municipal center. There, their spokesperson handed a letter to the municipality asking for subsidized housing. There was a great turnout.

Negotiations proceeded, which included getting the national education department to release the land to the local government, as well as a process for unemployed and low-income families to apply for a house in this new area. The negotiations took more than four years. These two issues – job training and housing – then came together with another new project.

Mthimkhulu (the great tree) and a job training center

In 2001, Nabs and Samkele had spotted another property in Kleinmond that was on the Main Road and was on the edge of the three racial areas – white, colored and black. This property was owned by a Jewish group that used it only during the holiday times for youth training. We did not know at this time that the training was for youth to be sent to Israel for their army. There had been some altercations between some of the Jewish youth and townspeople, and a rumor spread that they wanted to sell this land. This property had six buildings on it and was about 10 acres of land.

Nabs and Samkele took Anne and me over to the property. We went to the Great Tree that was in the center of this land. It had wonderful potential. We still had one of the blessed medals, so we buried it at the foot of the tree and blessed this space. Later I called one of Jewish board members and asked her if this land was for sale. She said they were open to selling it. Now the question was how to find the funds. There was a potential funder I was thinking about; however, the attack on the Twin Towers in New York City happened at that time. My potential funder got cold feet. So, this purchase was put on hold.

Several years later, another one of our funders was in Kleinmond, so we showed him this site and discussed the job training program with him. He was extremely positive and said yes to not only funding part of the purchase of this land, but he offered operating expenses for running job training programs with six staff. I then found four other funders from both South Africa and Europe to purchase the land and to support programs.

By 2007, we had taken over this land which we called Mthimkhulu. We decided on a launch and asked the Deputy President of South Africa, Phumzile Mlambo-Ngcuka, to give the main speech. Phumzile was a former student of Anne's in 1991 when Anne was teaching at the Adult Education Department at the University of Cape Town. She immediately said yes. We had hired six staff: two for setting up job training, two on the environment, one operational manager and promotions, and a part-time accountant.

As a team, we proceeded to promote this launch with people from all segments of the town, friends of the Grail, as well as government officials from the province and national office bearers. As the contractors renovated the office building and one classroom, they also built a stage next to the Great Tree and we also cleaned up the property from years of disuse. About one week before the public launch, I received a call from the Deputy President's office with three concerns. First, they wanted the Deputy President to fly into Kleinmond by helicopter. I immediately said no. I had remembered our Grail friend from Portugal (Maria de Lourdes) who told us stories of politicians who would helicopter into small towns and how this alienated the local people. They agreed not to fly in, but eventually came in a 7-car motorcade with sirens from Cape Town, which probably was more dangerous to regular traffic on the road.

The Deputy President's office also wanted their team to send 'food tasters' before the finger food would be served to guests right after the launch. Our caterer had these 'food tasters' in the kitchen with them, but they only just watched on and nibbled on items here and there. We had also been told that the bathroom next to the offices had to be a certain size for the Deputy President. The contractor obliged, but this seemed excessive to us.

The guests began to arrive and were finally joined by the Deputy President. Included in these guests were the Premier (Governor) of the Western Cape Province, several members of his cabinet including the Minister of Education, and the national cabinet Minister of Science and Technologies, Derek Hannekom. Anne had helped our team plan the program for the launch. After opening remarks by the Grail Board chair, Jewish, Christian, Muslim, and Xhosa (indigenous) blessings were given for the property. These ceremonies included children who had sprigs of leaves dipped in holy water to sprinkle through the earth and buildings. They were delighted to participate and brought energy to this event. Besides the Deputy President's speech and Anne's brief talk about what the Grail's mission was, the Premier of our Province spoke. In his statement he said that though he knew that the town wanted a high school in Kleinmond, this was not financially viable. However, he continued, there could be a vocation school here. I held onto this pledge, which would prove significant two years later.

I had been very focused on hiring program staff who were from Kleinmond, but I had not been focused on their skills sets, nor their understanding of the Training for Transformation approach to community participation or rolling out programs. This led to some significant tensions on the team. We did not have huge funds to implement programs, but enough to hire outside contractors to teach plumbing, electrical work, and building. Tensions simmered. After about a year, a few of these staff quit, including one due to increasing ill health.

I had recalled the Western Cape Premier's comment about the possibility of establishing a vocational school in Kleinmond and I called the Minister of Education, Cameron Dugmore, who had known of the Training for Transformation programs from years back in his work with Steve Biko. He came to discuss the possibilities. I later called him, and he whispered into his phone that he was in parliament but it was a boring debate, so would I text him. I did so and we more or less closed the deal via text messages. After a few months, we secured a vocational training school at Mthimkhulu. I sat on the interviewing panel and pushed for a woman to head it up who had been a secretary to an educational agency, as her passion for youth and education far outweighed that of some of the other candidates, one of whom had been a prison warden. No need to say more. The challenge was that this decision was made at the end of the year, and the Department gave us one week to recruit 100 students, all of whom had to be interviewed. We gathered all of our staff, including the ground staff at the Grail Center, to get people to apply. We succeeded and the vocational school opened at the beginning of the next year.

In South Africa, after ninth grade, students had to decide if they wanted to go to a university in the future and thus go to a regular high school, or whether they wanted to get a certificate for a trade and go to a vocational training school. There were two other vocational training sites in the district, but each meant students would have had to take a bus to that school. Local parents did not like this option, as going on a bus and waiting for a bus was also a site for selling drugs to their teenagers and possibly other criminal activity. One of the programs we instituted was meetings with parents. Although the school staff had meetings with parents, these were often about studying and how their kids were doing. Our program was about how to build smaller support groups with parents who had children with similar problems: concerns about drugs, relationships and the like. These support groups sometimes grew into neighborhood get-togethers and fostered community-building activities.

During this period, two other buildings were renovated: one as a computer classroom, for which I was able to get Dell Corporation in South Africa to donate 40 computers. Another building was renovated as a catering kitchen and dining room. The stage was set.

Within two years, this vocational school was awarded the highest marks in the Province. Mthimkulu had found its niche.

However, sadly, the government controlled the implementation of the Job Training program and certification of students. Often finances are given priority over mission. These job training programs were meant to be community-based educational institutions, thus drawing on families in close proximity. The government decided in 2016 to consolidate this Job Training program with another one of their programs in a town 30 miles away. The rationale was to save money. To me, this move came at a cost of providing education that is focused on the learner and is in keeping with the great adage of 'small is beautiful'. I regretted this move on many levels. Now placed in a holding position, the Grail continued with health care advocacy in the townships and an early learning center. As I write, the Department of Education has approached the Grail about purchasing this site for a high school. Another department is looking at the site for housing. So, the saga continues.

As I said earlier, the subsidized housing project in Kleinmond was starting to take shape, due to the work of the community development program and local activists. At the launch of Mthimkhulu, I also followed up with the national Minister of Science and Technologies, Derek Hanekom. Their department had a number of innovative projects for subsidized housing, in particular, incorporating different energy-efficient construction materials. A team from that department came to Mthimkhulu to see how their project could work on our site.

In our discussions, it was finally agreed that the Department would put up two new buildings on our site, one with conventional building materials and one with the innovative construction materials. We also got them to agree to building two housing units that would be examples of the subsidized houses to be built for the wider community. We had many meetings over the next two years about how to have more energy and water efficiency for the 411 houses to be built. Through this process, I learned a lot about not only new technologies, but when and how to make critical interventions. For me it was in keeping up good relationships with the leaders of such projects. The biggest winners, however, were the 411 families who gained safe, healthy homes to live in.

Spreading the message – *Training for Transformation*

In 2001, Anne and I were invited to Ireland to celebrate the Millennium with teams of people, globally, who were using *Training for Transformation*. Over 60 people attended from about 20+ countries. During one of the breaks, a Rwandan woman came to us and asked where they could get a longer training program, as they were not sure they had absorbed the essence of this work. They had been trained by so-and-so who was trained by someone else, and it was now fifth generation. Anne and I said we only knew of some universities who gave lectures on Paulo Freire's work, but no practical sessions. Then Anne and I looked at each other and said, 'Well, maybe we should set something up, as we now have a center to house such an effort.'

We pulled together seven women from Africa and Asia to discuss the endeavor. We developed a concept, and went to the director, Paddy Reilly, of the Institute for Social Development, which was housed on the property where this meeting was taking place. We asked Paddy if the Institute would accredit such a program – yes, he said, that would be great. We then announced that this one-year phased training would take place near Cape Town, South Africa in the near future. One of the African women, Adelina Mwau, and I went to Aachen, Germany where Misereor, a major funder of our work in the past, was located. They said yes to funding the trainings. Upon returning to South Africa, I wrote a funding proposal and sent it to a number of funders; within six months, we found six different funders to support the program.

We then sent the word out to those who had attended this meeting that the first *Training for Transformation* one-year phased training would begin in 2002. We hired Sr Rebecca Macugay, a Maryknoll Sister who had worked with us in Kenya, to be the coordinator of the program. Each of the two residential programs was to last eight weeks. Rather than building up a big staff, we hired a core team of three women. However, for each one-week module, we would bring in a specialist on such topics as development, Freire's methods of critical consciousness, group processes, spirituality, economics, gender, advocacy, and organizational development with strategic planning. A number of the specialists were willing to work with us pro bono and some even paid for their own transport.

Along with Ina Conradie from the University of the Western Cape who had worked with Anne on these methods, we developed a rough curriculum for each week, that we sent to the Institute of Development Studies in Ireland. So the work included getting the funding, developing a curriculum, resourcing part-time staff, recruiting participants, and the ever-present burden of getting visas for all the participants. We were also convinced we wanted only teams from each country, who could then return home to work together. Doing so, we hoped, would ensure that if a person dropped out for family or work reasons, the program would continue in their country. We also asked that each participant had full approval from their organization stating they would use this program within their own work in communities with which they worked back home.

Because the participants came from training organizations that worked on organizing grassroots communities, we scheduled the two sets of the two-month residential sessions to happen in two different years. We thought this would give the organizations and participants more accountability to their organizations. The first year we had teams from 11 different countries. The mix was wonderful. As the Center had 2 and 3 bedroomed houses, we were able to mix the nationalities of the people in each house. This of course sometimes caused cross-cultural tensions, and so in plenary sessions, we had to deal with coming to common understandings between cultures.

During the two months of living and working together, breakfasts, lunches, and suppers along with teas were catered for the whole group during the week. But as participants lived in houses with kitchens, we decided to give each household an allowance for purchasing their food for the weekends. The shops were only five blocks away. We had an assignment over the weekend before the environmental week module. Each household needed to find out the geographical source of every item of food they purchased for that one weekend. On Monday, each household reported the total number of kilometers their food had travelled. For the whole group this often ranged from 60,000 to 75,000 kilometres. We would then discuss what foods could have been produced locally or nearby and the cost and pollution of fuel to transport the foods to our town. This was an eye-opener for all of us.

The Training for Transformation program has a deep value that the training is not just developing a practical skill set to animate communities for actions or provide insights into the root causes of the issues communities face, but also how to enable participants to be committed to justice over the long haul – their lifetime. A one-week module for each residential part of the program was dedicated to enabling participants to reflect on their faith calling. This basic value has sustained the program for over 40 years as of this writing.

As this program recruited teams from a number of countries and organizations, the religious backgrounds of participants was found to be very diverse. In the first year of the program, a team of three women from a refugee organization in the United States attended. One was Christian, one Buddhist and one Muslim. Each morning, a team would lead a meditation session. In December 2002, one team led a meditation on the birth of Jesus. Their meditation question for the group was what we thought about the role of Mary. By this time, the group was quite sensitive to the different religious backgrounds of us all. After a very long silence about this question about Mary, the Muslim woman, Sumaya Karimi, stated quite strongly that Mary was the strongest woman in the history of our world. She said something like, can you imagine being the mother of a revolutionary? Can you imagine how she felt as he was being tortured and then killed? She needs to be our model of being a strong woman. This left many of us breathless.

At the end of the second residential phase, Sumaya came to me and said that being at the Grail Center and in this program had restored her own faith. She told me her father was a direct descendant of the prophet Mohammed. The family lived in Afghanistan and her father was opposed to the Taliban. The Taliban had targeted him to be killed so he fled to the mountains and took Sumaya with him for a year where she studied the Koran and learned from her father. He was then told that it was safe for him to return to Kabul, which they did. Within months, he was assassinated and their family fled to the USA. For Sumaya to regain her faith at the Grail Center and in this program was, for me, one of the highest tributes that could be paid to the generative force of our learning and growing and healing together.

In 2007 when the second residential program was to begin, a major massacre and rebellion took place in Kenya. I had just been at a conference with funders in Johannesburg where I met a woman who was doing major trauma healing in communities. While talking with her, I thought it could be very useful to the participants coming to the second residential program to have some time for healing. Although not all of our core staff agreed, we brought this specialist to the first week when all the participants returned for this second phase. The focus on trauma opened up many wounds that participants from countries other than Kenya had experienced as well. Liberians and Rwandans had experienced major deaths in the uprisings and genocide in their countries. Women had also experienced domestic abuse. What was important for me was that this trauma facilitator was able to open up these traumas, have them articulated, and then move participants into a healing and nurturing space.

During the last week of the second residential program, we focused on planning for their work back home. How to do strategic planning versus just 'planning'? This was critically important as practice was key to learning and internalizing their newer insights and theories. I took leadership on these sessions and had the group go into small groups of 5, with each group being given a set of pick-up sticks. Each group had to pick up every stick without moving another stick – if another stick was moved, they had to start again. As they went around the circle to make their one move each person had to say out loud *why* they were making this particular move. One person from this small group was asked to stand outside the group and be an observer. The observer would write down what each person said about their move and their justification.

This exercise would run for about 15-20 minutes. Then, when all the groups came back together, one or two comments from the observers would be recorded on newsprint. What was amazing was that almost everything we knew about developing a 'strategy' and the need for strategic planning was brought forth from the group.

When this was completed, I would put participants in 'home groups' in either the same organization, country, or common work to reflect on these learnings regarding what they might be doing already, what they thought they neeeded to change or add, or even mistakes they had made in the past. This process worked like a charm in moving participants from simply planning to planning strategically.

As the residential part of the Training for Transformation program only took place over two months within a calendar year, programmatically and financially, this meant we did not need full time staff all year long. We agreed that the core team would be present throughout the eight weeks. We therefore had three core staff members. Their work throughout the year was divided into recruitment of new participants, mentoring and following up of participants and sending organizations the plans for work back home, solidifying resource staff for the next residential program, dealing with finances, visas, and many more tasks. The core staff were also facilitators of two or more modules.

One of the best initiatives was to bring in some very experienced facilitators as resource staff for a week. The themes were spirituality, gender, ecology, economics, conflict resolution, culture, group process, and later organizational development. Anne and I would often go to some of these sessions to keep abreast of new information methods. Later when some men were brought into the program, the gender module included both a male and female facilitator, when the group would be separated by gender at times. Quite a dynamic, as one can imagine.

Most important was finding strong, competent, and committed leadership for this program. Ntombi Nyathi had been in exile from Zimbabwe and was a participant in the 2004 diploma course. We asked her to be on the local community development staff. In 2010 we asked her to be the director of the Training for Transformation program, and she has expanded and developed the program with great energy and insights.

Think Wells. After a year of implementing this program, we thought it would be a good idea to bring in some of the staff from the Irish Institute for Social Development, some participants, a number of resource people and others in this field. We did extra fund raising for this 8-day conversation. At first, we called it a 'Think Tank', then Sr Becky Macugay suggested calling it a 'Think Well'. This title could be thought of in a number of ways from fresh water to 'thinking well'. Everyone was quite inspired by it, so much so that we instituted Think Wells every other year with different themes. One was with practitioners from Latin America and other geographic areas and disciplines that ensured this program in the future. Another Think Well was on the new economics with the increased influence of China in Africa and globally. This was called 'A New Map of the World', and we brought in an expert from the Tony Blair Foundation. When the global recession took place in 2008, we focused a Think Well on the economic crisis and its effects on countries of the South. Resource people included African economists and trade union organizers. Another Think Well was implemented on the climate crisis.

In 2013, one of our funders and the publisher of the *Training for Transformation* volumes (Practical Action Publishing out of the E. F. Schumacher Institute) were urging Anne and me to write a new book on the outcomes of the Training for Transformation programs globally. We said we were not the right people to write it; however, if the funder would pay for 36+ invited practitioners to come to the

Grail Center for 10 days, we would get this book written. The funding came through.

Training for Transformation in Practice became the title of the book that ensued from our gathering. The first three days we had discussions on new layers of consciousness. Anne and I had already written the introduction. We only had about 17,000 words remaining for the entire book and were worried that there would be too many chapters. On the fourth day, we asked the group who would like to develop together an impact evaluation tool and who would like to write a chapter. Thank the Lord, the group split in half. Anne and I took the group who would write their chapter to the library.

As we sat in a circle, I asked that each person to write the theme of their chapter. Then I asked, what is the title for your chapter; what is the sub-title for your chapter; and finally, what is the *sub*-subtitle of your chapter. We then went around the circle with people sharing what they had written, with others asking questions, making comments and working towards clarification. We then gave this group three days in which to complete the writing of their chapter. We also stressed that they could go to anyone in the room as a mentor. They had completely free time, punctuated with breaks for meals with the other group members.

This worked, with all but one chapter completed on time. I learned from this that a carrot and a stick both work. The carrot was a free trip to Cape Town for 10 days near the ocean. The stick was that if their chapter was not turned in after three days and on time, they would have to walk to the airport which was a one-hour drive away. Of course, no one really believed the latter, but they also realized that they had an obligation to get the task accomplished. *Training for Transformation in Practice* was published six months later.

This autobiography is not the place to write a long litany of the impact of my works and especially of Training for Transformation, which could be the work of a number of dissertations. The Freire method is sometimes called the psycho-social method. To us, this meant transformation on many levels: oneself, a small group or team, an organization or institution, the wider society and the environment or cosmos. A number of these impacts are recorded in *Training for Transformation in Practice*. Training for Transformation programs are now delivered in 61 countries and implemented by over 100 non-profits organizations. Following up with each is the new direction, led by the director, Ntombi Nyathi.

There have been changes to the program. After a major evaluation by one funder, Misereor, in 2016-17, a shift in approach to broader and more local communities was adopted. The one-year diploma course reached about 20 organizations each year. The positive side of the longer course was that the skills and insights went into depth. It also enabled participants to gain strong friendships across cultures and borders and deepened their long-term commitment to social justice. The downside was many organizations could not afford to release their staff for such a long period of time, and the risk of these staff finding different jobs or vocations.

As of 2020, the Training for Transformation program will be regionalized with a certificate. The courses will be run for 2 or 3 weeks in phases that will result in many more organizations gaining the ability to change their practices to be more effective in mobilizing communities. Of course, making this change has risks, but it is worth the effort to broaden the base of work and will hopefully reach and meet the needs of more disenfranchised people.*

*See Appendix: Letting go as a founder, for my reflections on the lessons I have learnt from the Training for Transformation program over the years.

A summary of my work in South Africa – and what I learned

The following is a list of the work I did in South Africa over these years. With my central theme of 'being productive', this is rather amazing to me.

SOUTH AFRICA: 1995-2014 and continues

Founder:	Gender Advocacy Project
Founder:	Fair Share (economic literacy with local activists)
Co-founder:	Grail Retreat and Conference Center purchased
Co-founder:	AIDS Response
Founder:	Local Community Development Program
Founder:	Job Training Center purchased
Founder:	Job Training programs implemented
Funding:	411 subsidized houses with solar hot water and water storage
Co-founder:	International Training for Transformation one-year diploma
	Continues with 61 countries implementing programs

How could all of this work thrive? In hindsight I think it is what Anne and I learned in Kenya and that is finding solid, committed leadership locally or within the project itself. I was not central to the work after a few years in any of these programs. Both Anne and I believed our work was to work ourselves out of a job. In the words of Lao Tzu:

> Go to the people,
> Live with them, love them
> And of the best leaders
> The people will say,
> We did this ourselves.

Obviously, over 20 years changes have occurred. This is inevitable. Our world, local communities and leadership keep changing to reflect the needs of the times. The ongoing work with each of these programs does continue. Some projects merged with other groups, one program became more local in its efforts, and some are in transition to different ways of addressing their missions.

How was it possible to start so many programs that continue to the date of this writing? There are several things to note. Anne had an intuitive sense of spotting leadership. Much of our work was done with groups, whether locally, in provinces or national workshops. We did many sessions of group processes, feedback on leadership styles and building trust in groups; these can all be found in Book 2 of *Training for Transformation*. Spotting potential leadership in the participants in these workshops was essential. Was the participant open to feedback? Were they asking substantive questions that helped a group to go deeper into an issue? How did they treat other members in their team efforts?

In the midst of these years of facilitating workshops, I also read a book called *Leadership Without Easy Answers* by Ronald A. Heifetz (a psychiatrist at the John F. Kennedy School of Government). He emphasized the ability of a leader to 'hold' a group. I understood 'holding' to mean to help people understand each other, to find compromises, to feel they could live with their decisions, even if not their own opinions, and to encourage the group to act on their own, with their own leadership. This meant building teams. A metaphor Heifetz used was that a group is like a dance. The leader is on the dance floor with the group. Then the leader goes to a balcony to watch the patterns and tries to see and understand the whole. The leader then goes back to the dance floor, and using his/her insights, to ensure that the dance is in harmony and being enjoyed.

My deepest learning is about how to let go and when. I found that when the leadership of a project begins to assert their own authority and demonstrates capacity to win the affection of those with whom they work, it is a great time to let go completely. There were times when new leadership took a direction that I may have thought was too 'narrow' or not deep enough, and I regretted their decisions, but those were their decisions based on what they saw on the ground. So be it. Humbling as it may be, I know that deep down I certainly do not have The Answer. (Well, most of the time!)

My personal life over those 20 years in South Africa

Anne and I were two strong women. When we moved into our new house we both agreed that we needed two more rooms for guests and offices, as I would most likely work mainly from home. We were building our new home, together. This common task helped us to bridge the separations that had lasted for more than seven years. Although the addition to our house took months and was sometimes quite noisy, we found delight in a new venture together.

Anne understood I needed to have a compelling work that was mine, and not built on her vision. She had started a women's training program that she had handed over to a team and she then worked with a team on development education at the University of the Western Cape. I had found funding for Fair Share; we were finding new ways to 'be together'. We both would bounce ideas off each other, and encouraged and affirmed each other. As I had always trusted Anne's instincts, her affirmations spurred me on with more confidence.

Anne had been in therapy with an excellent therapist. I decided I would also have some sessions with this therapist separately. We also had some common sessions. One of my main learnings from this was how our different birth experiences were important to building our new relationship. While Anne was still in her mother's womb, her mother had an appendix operation, thus a trauma to this unborn child. I, on the other hand as described earlier, came into this world feeling 'safe'. I may have unconsciously understood this difference and my way to support Anne was to join her in *her* vision. Now we needed to find a way for us both to become our authentic Selves. During these years, Anne continued to be on the Grail board but more important for her was focusing on becoming a contemplative. She was in walking groups, contemplative meditation groups, participated in study groups of other religions and had different friends. I was living out my need to be 'productive', as written about earlier regarding the organizations and work I helped initiate.

Anne and I had learned to laugh at ourselves with another difference between us. I am a problem-solver and always think that there are 100 ways to solve any problem. If a criticism or problem occurred, Anne would usually think that it was something she did 'wrong'. An example of this would be when we were driving in our car and someone beeped their horn. Anne would say, 'Oh look out.' And I would say, 'No, they are beeping at someone else, not us.' We had a good laugh about this difference.

In 1997, during a routine mammogram, they spotted shadows on two sides of my breast. My surgeon recommended a total mastectomy. When I called friends and a doctor in the USA, they said that total mastectomies were usually not done anymore. Anne and I went to an oncologist at the University. She was an older woman who seemed very wise. I asked her what she would do if in my place, and she said she would choose a total mastectomy as one couldn't know what was in between the two spots. Then Anne asked, what would this choice do for me, psychologically. The oncologist said, 'It depends on how you see yourself: from the inside or the outside.' That did it for me, for of course I saw myself from the inside. I immediately called the surgeon and scheduled my operation. As we had not had lunch, Anne and I went to a café on the ocean and ate our lunch on the rocks watching the waves; and Anne said the Psalms, by heart. We celebrated this moment. I have been cancer free since that operation.

By 2010 and after we had started the Training for Transformation international training program, the Grail board felt it was time for me to hand over the overall directorship of all of the programs. We did a search for this new director and hired a person who had been using these methods in her own work as a group therapist and who also trained others in them. At a rather contentious board meeting, I was told to go on a holiday for a long time to give space to the new director. I was also told not to talk to the new director, even though I might be on the same property at the same time as she was. I knew that it would take months to hand over the fundraising relationships to the new director, and I said so. Some members did not accept this. Several meetings took place to sort it out, but to no one's satisfaction.

One board member said that nothing can grow under two strong trees. I later took a walk in our sacred forest in the Grail Center and saw two strong trees and lo and behold, there were at least three other types of trees growing right beside the two big trees. Anne and I took a three-day retreat in Cape Town, and Anne wrote the following, which expressed most of where, at least the two of us were.

> Long, long ago, in a semi-arid land two tree seeds were blown onto the soil. Struggling to find nurture, they found some fertile land and small water streams that gave them strength to grow. Soon their roots became strong, their branches multiplied, and they grew taller and taller. Over time, other seeds were dropped from their leaves, and slowly took root, but of course, were in the shade of the two parent trees.

> Some of these latecomers grew – finding their way to the waters and light. Others were not as lucky and were dwarfed by the shade of the two mighty oaks. The mighty oaks grew, despite the storms that tore off some branches, or dry seasons that slowed them up. Often, they needed to be pruned, to allow people to walk beneath them, or branches cut to allow other parts to become strong.

> One day, a new farmer looked at the oaks and thought that these oaks were of no use. The latecomer-trees were not growing as fast as they could to form a plantation. The aim of course, was to replicate the oaks. The solution was clear, as the old oaks could not be transplanted, they needed to be cut down so other oaks could grow.

As the tree cutter was preparing his machines to cut them down, the birds who had built their houses in the two oaks for years, started a riot of protest. The wild grasses nearby started to wave their blades. The aloes and flowers that had been nurtured in the mulch at the base of the oaks knew they would be no more. Sensitive plants that needed the shade to grow in their own way, not just like the oaks, shuddered The bushes that drew their sustenance from the two oaks were worried that they would be replaced.

Hearing the cry of the birds, the wind whistling through the bushes, and seeing the bright colors of the flowers at the base of the two oaks, the tree cutter sat and pondered. The tree cutter saw that although the trees were old, they still bore acorns and sprouted new leaves. The tree cutter wondered whether replicating more oaks was the only way to make a beautiful and fruitful space. The two oaks did give this place character. The two oaks did give a home to the birds who plant the seeds of other fruits just nearby. The two oaks did have flowerbeds at their base. The two oaks have given delight to people to revel in their shade and dream new dreams. Do I really need to replicate these two oaks?

The tree cutter looked around and in delight, saw some new open spaces that had not been tilled. Perhaps the saplings of these tall trees could be planted in that ground. Or why not fruit trees that could nurture the people in different ways? The needs of the area were great. Why be so focused on replicating this space (which was only in the mind) for the same things? An interchange and cross-fertilization – with the help of those wise bees and birds to bring communication to the whole was possible.

The tree cutter wondered whether those who benefited from the presence of the two oaks (the birds, the flowers and wild grasses and bushes) could not gain from a diversity of trees in different ways. Is a diverse plethora of species as important to our earth as a plantation of replicated trees? And why have I thought that only oak trees are more important to the earth than fruit trees, scrubs, flowers or grass?

Maybe not all is lost by having two tall oaks.

Sadly, this experience ended with the new director resigning, along with several of the board members.

One of the community development staff members was Ntombi Nyathi. Ntombi was from Zimbabwe and had been in the 2004 one-year Training for Transformation program. She had, and still has, a deep spiritual calling and had integrated the participatory approach of Training for Transformation to her work. With a new board formed, we asked Ntombi if she would take on the directorship of the Training for Transformation program. At the same time, we found a new manager for the Grail Center.

Ntombi said yes to this new position, but was hesitant about doing the fund raising. I said I would walk with her and I asked her to take one of the last funding proposals I had written and adapt it to her words and the work she wanted to focus on for the next three years. She then met with her team and did just that and passed it back to me. This back and forth between us went on for several months. I also introduced her through international telephone calls and face-to-face visits with our funders. By this time, Ntombi had hit her stride. She told me that I had taken her to a cliff and pushed her off, and she learned she could fly.

My need to be 'productive' meant that my quiet time was attached to 'doing something'. I found I also was a bit bored with group discussions (as Anne also had become). So quiet space was what I relished, yet very differently from Anne, I needed to be productive. I learned from a handyman how to restore furniture like those who restored antiques. This was a quiet time as I did not use an electric sander. I also sanded and varnished window frames at home and at the Grail Center. Living near the ocean meant that the air was salty and wooden window frames needed work very often. What fun!

My mother was now living in a retirement home in my hometown of Oconomowoc, Wisconsin, USA. Every two years, I would make the trip to see my mom. My aunt was in the same retirement home, but had become quite irritable. My mother was now in her nineties, and was becoming more and more quiet. I would take her down to the lake in her wheelchair, where she sat serenely, looking at the sky and the land while I read a book. We both enjoyed these times together. I came back home, to Cape Town, and said to Anne that there must be some things one can do to not become irritable in our older years. 'I want to become serene,' I said. Anne looked at me straight in the eye and said, 'Sally, I do not think that is in your character.' Oh my. I thought about this for a long time, and a few months later said to Anne that I would try to become more kind. This really is an action – a way of 'doing' rather than 'being', and perhaps something that will help in my older years.

Anne would often find moments for celebrations. She decided on an all-day bash at the Grail Center for her seventieth birthday. She planned a morning reflection with her favorite poems and readings, and a lunch. I suggested we also have a place for people to share together. What I had in mind was to produce a video with pictures of Anne and her family and our work along with my voice-over narrative and music from the New World Symphony. At Christmas time, about two months before her birthday, we went to the Grail Center for a one-week holiday and I took all her photo albums with me. I mentioned to Anne that it was time to organize all of these pictures. I asked her many questions and secretly went into another room and took notes for my voice over on the video. This was fun to make with the help of a friend who had the technical skills. On the afternoon of her party, I showed the video and Anne was delighted with my birthday present to her.

That same year I celebrated my sixtieth birthday and we held my party at our timeshare at Monkey Valley. Many guests arrived and I was in the middle of doing the budget work in Fair Share. Anne then read to me and guests from her version of *The Little Prince*. Here are a few lines that had us all in an uproar of laughter.

'... five-hundred-and-one millions ----' the businessman said to the Little Prince.

'Millions of what?' replied the Little Prince.

'Millions of those little objects, which one sometimes sees in the sky.'...

'Ah! You mean the stars?' said the Little Prince

'Yes' replied the businessman ...

'What do you do with these stars?' asked the Little Prince.

'Nothing. I own them ... I count them and recount them. I am a man who is naturally interested in matters of consequence ... Then I write the number of stars on a little paper and put this in a drawer and lock it with a key.'

Said the businessman.

...'I own a flower which I water every day. It is of some use to my flower, that I own it. But you are of no use to the stars.' On matters of consequence, the little prince had ideas which were very different from those of the grown-ups ... The grown-ups are certainly altogether extraordinary.

Some most enjoyable moments during these years was taking Anne's dog Copper for daily walks. Cape Town is in one of the most beautiful locations for a city; it has the sea, mountains, parks and forests. Sometimes Anne had to drag me away from my computer or phone for our walk with Copper. Sometimes we went to a nearby park, or a forest and often to the beach five minutes away from our home. These were often the times we talked about what was in our hearts. Sometimes it meant chasing after Copper, but all with good humor. For this I remain grateful.

Move to Kleinmond

Our work at the Grail Center in Kleinmond was keeping us there more than in Cape Town. At the same time, Anne's great-nephew, Benjy, was about to get married to Romy, a childhood sweetheart. We thought we would keep the Cape Town house in the family, and move to Kleinmond. We had a plot next to the Grail Center and had built a 3-bedroom home there. The house in Cape Town and the houses we built in Kleinmond came from inheritances from two of my aunts who did not have children. They willed enough money to purchase or build these houses. Also building is quite cheap in South Africa compared to countries in the North. This of course took some logistics to move, and we had help from the relatives, but it worked. A year later, as we had a second plot on the edge of the Grail Center, we decided to build two smaller houses there. These would be for Anne's family to visit, and the Center could rent it out for their own programs and others. Again, what fun for me to build some more houses. My grandfather was working full-time in me!

During this time, Anne fulfilled her passion of working in the Sacred Forest, pruning and gardening, becoming part of spiritual groups in the area and of course now walking our two dogs: Casper and Pippa. I continued to help when asked, with the Training for Transformation program and Mthimkhulu.

Coming to the USA in 2013,
and Pilgrim Place in 2014

In 2013, the International Grail decided to hold a two-week-long celebration of Grail members aged 70-100. Members from all of the twenty-one countries were invited. Anne and I decided to go, and 70 members attended. There were few actual programs, but we filled up our time with common discussions and sharing of concerns. As the international Grail had also been holding meetings for younger members of the Grail, the global and some USA Grail members aged 50-70, felt they were being left out. So, they arranged an informal weekend near the conference center where we were meeting. Anne was asked to give a talk about our 70-100 meeting on the weekend to bring the 50-70-year-olds up to speed. To the delight of all of us, she started her talk by saying how when we arrived, some of us whispered to a friend and pointed to someone and asked, now remind me, who is that? Then we would go and greet this person and say 'Oh, you haven't changed a bit!' On a deeper level this was true.

A Grail friend of Anne's since 1954, Donna Ambrogi, invited Anne to travel to California to the retirement community called Pilgrim Place. Twenty years earlier, I had been to Pilgrim Place and had put my name on a waiting list. I wanted to visit my hometown after this meeting so Anne flew off to Pilgrim Place and I went to Oconomowoc. Donna wined and dined Anne. We then met up and flew back to Cape Town.

Upon our return, the Grail Center Manager came to us to say she wanted to move back to Cape Town as they missed the city and their relatives. She was handing in her resignation. After she left, Anne turned to me and said, 'We are moving to Pilgrim Place.' I was taken aback. I had earlier decided that I would not try to persuade Anne that we should move to the USA. But here it was – a flat out statement. Anne also said we would not tell anyone of this decision until after her family reunion at Christmas time, six months later. We then applied to Pilgrim Place, had a Skype interview with the applications committee, and were accepted. Donna then said to us that in order for Anne to enter the United States with a Green Card, we needed to get married. We had now been (more or less) together 44 years. As we were not telling anyone about our departure, Anne said we could not sell our house in Kleinmond until after the Christmas family reunion. Being a forward planner, I went to an estate agent in Kleinmond and said that we would be selling our house, but only in the new year. There could be no signs or announcements about the sale of our house.

Anne and I proceeded to the family reunion in Bloemfontein (about a 2-hour flight from Cape Town), with Anne going earlier to Johannesburg to tell the Grail members there of our decision. We shared our decision with the family, and continued to have outings, swimming and lovely meals and sharing together. Upon return to Kleinmond, I went to the estate agent and she said she had a buyer for our house. I was very surprised and slightly worried. She had a couple from Cape Town who were about to retire, and so she had showed them our house and they loved it. Within a week, our house was sold, but we were told we would not have to move out until October, which gave us breathing space. At the same time, the buyers wanted any and all furniture, appliances, and anything else we wished to sell them. What a gift.

Now we had to figure out getting married. We found that only one minister, a Unitarian who had previously been the mayor of Cape Town, could legally preform same-sex marriages. We went and talked with him and set a date to have a ceremony in our old house in Cape Town with four friends as witnesses. Before we could have the ceremony, we had to go to the South African offices of Home Affairs to get legal permission to marry. Off we went to this dark building and up to the fifth floor to an empty large waiting room. There we sat. Two young African men came out to greet us and ushered us into two separate rooms to be interviewed. Neither of us knew what to expect. Basically, they each just wanted our histories. After these interviews we went back to the waiting room and they both came out and said to us, 'Why did you wait so long?' We all laughed, talked a bit about the laws, and got our marriage certificate within a month.

Our marriage ceremony was simple. Anne took her nephew's arm and walked down from the second floor, and I walked behind them. We exchanged vows (that I do not remember) and were pronounced married. We then had some food together with our four witnesses and Benjamin and Romy who now lived in our old house. In some ways it was a 'marriage of convenience' though we knew we had our primary relationship to the end, for better or worse, in sickness and in health.

However, we still had to apply for Anne's green card for her to enter the United States. We went to the US Consulate in Cape Town and were told only Embassies do that transaction, so we had to go to Johannesburg. They had given us the paperwork to fill in, which became a file about two inches thick when completed. It included photographs of us together from our first year together, our financial situation, our marriage certificate from South Africa, documents that we had signed together ... and on and on.

We got to our 1 o'clock appointment at the USA Embassy in Johannesburg to find there were fifty other people with 1 o'clock appointments. We were now seasoned waiters and were the second-to-last people called to a window with a black South African woman who went through our papers, continuing to say, no, this isn't right, no, no. I had spent hours getting all the papers correct, and finally she said we need to see a person in the next window. We waited. When we were called to this next window, a young woman greeted us and I detected a USA Midwest accent. So, we chatted about Minnesota and Wisconsin. She looked through our photographs and said, 'This is so romantic!' A good start. Then she said Anne was missing police clearance from Uganda and Kenya. One needed police clearance from all countries where one had lived for over six months. Anne in her gracious voice said, she had left Uganda just before Idi Amin took over as president, and most likely all of the papers there were in a mess. The Embassy officer said she would go talk to her supervisor. When she returned, she said those police clearances were waived. Anne would get her green card. Our lives had continually been beleaguered with getting the right papers to stay in any country where we lived. This entrance visa now had worked.

For six months, we continued to hand over work to the board and staff. We had boxes in our third bedroom that we would take to the States. We had hired a mover. We asked three of Anne's great nephews and niece (Benjy, Themba, and Puleng) to come for a weekend before we flew off to the USA on Monday evening. The moving company had taken the 26 boxes and three small pieces of furniture to ship to California. The new owners were keeping the big furniture. We wanted the kids to have many of the kitchen items and linens. They drew numbers and later said they had only disagreed about the wine glasses. We drove that night to the airport and the grandnephews and niece saw us off with great gusto.

Settling into the United States
Dear friend Barbara Troxell and her husband, Gene, picked us up at Los Angeles airport. All of a sudden, we were on eight-laned freeways and weaving between traffic. We had been told by Pilgrim Place that a house would be ready for us in the first half of the year. It was now July 29, 2014 and there was still no house. There were fifteen Grail members living at Pilgrim Place and between Donna and Barbara, they found a house where the residents were on a 3-month summer holiday. There was a lovely backyard, so we often lived outside. The Grail gave us a big welcoming supper the next evening.

A unique feature of Pilgrim Place is that all residents eat a full course meal at noon every day. You pay for it whether you eat there or not, so more than 200 residents eat together. The dining room staff have the names of the residents on small plastic name places, and each day, with the help of a computer system, your place at a seven-person round table is changed. Over a period of time, you most likely have sat at this noon meal with everyone on campus. This prevents cliques and builds relationships with everyone. Another part of the noon meal, besides someone offering a prayer, are announcements. These announcements can be quite creative and add some humor to our day. As one resident said, these noon meals bring us outside of ourselves, which adds to our health and well-being.

By September we still did not have a house we could move into. Though a house was now designated for us, it needed its 10-year upgrade. Anne and I decided on having a wall between the kitchen and dining room knocked down and we added an outside deck. Enjoying such construction, I went to our 'new' house daily to watch the progress. It was slow. We then moved into someone else's apartment for two weeks, another person's apartment for a month, and one final place for the last two weeks. By mid-November we had moved into our new abode.

Residents do a lot of volunteer work for each other and our community as a whole. There is a team that helps residents move. Our twenty-six boxes had arrived in late October and were stored in an empty house on campus. On moving day, six residents moved those boxes, and the used furniture we had purchased from previous residents, into the new space. This was completed within an hour. I had organized about ten women to unpack the boxes, wash the dishes, put everything away in cupboards and make our beds. Before lunchtime, we were settled and there was not a box in sight. On Thanksgiving Day, we had a blessing of our home with friends.

Another unique feature of Pilgrim Place is that the residents themselves develop and implement programs with each other. There is no hired 'program director'. There are over 30 committees to do this work, which spans from running the microphones for lectures, arranging concerts, organizing meetings, holding once-a-week evening vespers, lining up Saturday night movies, etc. to decorating tables for special occasions. Anne and I had joined a number of these activities to find our separate and common niches. Pilgrim Place also holds a 'festival' open to the public each year. There are over sixty booths selling everything from used books, furniture, household goods, weaving items, stained glass, pottery, plants, jams and marmalades made from produce grown on campus, as well as two food cafes. The funds collected from the festival goes to an endowment to pay for residents who may run out of money near the end of their lives. Over 10,000 people come to the festival and we raise about $200,000 net each year for this endowment each year. It is another means of building our community.

For the next six months, we continued to learn about this intentional community, going to free concerts at one of the five colleges in the town of Claremont, or going into Los Angeles to the famous Walt Disney Concert Hall with friends. Anne had fallen earlier in the year and broken her wrist, so we had to learn the very complicated health care system in the United States. We were very fortunate that Donna Ambrogi was very concerned that Anne, as a green card holder but not an original United States citizen, get on the national health insurance system called Medicare. She was very concerned and had called numerous offices, even in Washington DC and had finally found a clause in the regulations that would allow Anne to be on Medicare. Within days of our arrival in August 2014, Donna took us to the nearby Social Security office and when we got to the official, Donna was into her persuasive speech. After a few moments the official said, 'Oh, I just had a case like this last week. No problem, it is fine.' We all breathed a sigh of relief.

In June, Anne said to me that we needed to have a heart-to-heart talk about how we wanted to be here. I agreed but we didn't set time aside. In July, Anne had a regular colonoscopy exam where they found cancerous polyps. Anne had had colon cancer in South Africa, had some of her colon taken out and her tests before we left South Africa showed her as being cancer free. This was therefore a shock to us. That same night, she got sick and we went to the Emergency Room and she was operated on immediately. She returned home in three days. Our heart-to-heart talk was now delayed as we got focused on her health.

By September Anne was feeling she was healing and we both started entering into the events and work within this community. In October, we went to an oncologist who told us that Anne's blood tests showed the readings for the presence of cancer had changed from 3 (something) in July to 34 in October. We realized this was her death notice. We came home and were quiet – not knowing at all what to say and just held each other for hours.

The festival was upon us, so Anne went to the area to sell plants, but needed a ride to one block away. By the middle of November, she was sick again and was back in the hospital. I also got the flu so Barbara stayed with Anne and when she was to be released back home, Barbara got her into our Pilgrim Place skilled nursing facility on the property. Anne asked for the hospice doctor and we now were in the last period of her life. I spent all of my time with Anne and often sitting in a garden just outside her room, reading out loud to her from books she loved.

She then asked me to arrange for the 'last rites' to be given to her on Thanksgiving Day by a priest living there and with friends present. The room was packed; Anne had planned the whole ritual and officiated from her bed. She had chosen beautiful readings and songs. A resident poet read her own poem written for Anne at this moment.

NO STRANGE LAND

I will not die
in a strange land
Death is common
to every country
and clime
and I have befriended
this amazing planet
in its totality
Every part of it
is beautiful
every valley precious
all the mountains
I have climbed
have claimed me
And the people
the dear many people

of my well-traveled life
walk beside me
day by day
family and friends
lovers companions
co-workers
even those
I cannot name
accompany me
on this lovely
flower-bedecked trail
I will not die
in a strange land
There are love songs
in the rain showers
in the flow of rivers
in the linked arms
of all I meet
There is familiarity
and friendship
and wonder-filled expectation
in the joy of living fully
from birth to transition
There is no strange land
for me to die in anymore
No one is a stranger
Everywhere is home.

Pat Patterson, 25 November 2015

The following day, I gathered up my courage and asked Anne what she would like at her memorial service, as memorial services are held for all residents and is a tradition at Pilgrim Place. Before I could get paper and pen in hand, Anne rattled off numerous readings and songs.

Days later Anne she was moved home and a hospital bed replaced her own. One day while I was in another room, Anne yelled out, 'Oh, and also E.E. Cummings!' I knew exactly which poem she also wanted in her memorial. I pulled together a small group of Grail members and friends to arrange her memorial service here at Pilgrim Place.

Anne's relatives from Zimbabwe and China now arrived, one by one. Her nephew, John Stewart, read Shakespeare and other poems and stories to her. Then her niece Alice Hootsman arrived from China, followed later by her husband Bert. They sang Christmas carols and played Scrabble. I think Anne still won. Kathy Stewart then arrived and helped with readings and sitting by Anne's bedside. I seemed to get 'busy' with arrangements of nurses, food, and medications. Of course, I regret I took too much time doing these mundane things. The hospice nurse came two days before Anne died and told us Anne had no blood pressure, and she was in her last stage. Kathy spent two nights by her bedside. In Anne's last hours, in the early morning of 26 December, I held her hand as she transitioned into another life.

I called Barbara Troxell and the funeral home to come pick up her body. Barbara called Grail members and friends. I put on the music of Fauré's 'Requiem' and we listened in silence. When her body was moved to the vehicle, we said a hallelujah. I had decided I would take three days of silence so friends hosted Kathy who was still here. I listened to music, re-read Anne's autobiography and poetry, and remembered her. I also wrote to friends and relatives in South Africa, the USA and around the world of our beloved Anne's death.

I wanted to get away for a while so went to Cincinnati to be with my dear friend, Nancy Richardson. It was a consoling and easy time with Nancy and her partner Elaine. Both Nancy and I were on a Grail committee to sell part of the land at Grailville. We set up a meeting with our committee and tagged it on to a meeting of local Grail members and friends to discuss the sale. This face-to-face meeting with our committee was a real coming together of lovely women and set the stage for our continued work through conference phone calls for the next four and half years. The meeting with local folks did not resolve their major concern, which was not to sell the land.

Back at Pilgrim Place, Anne's memorial was prepared and held in mid-January. Besides the preludes of Beethoven and Mozart's piano music, we listened to 'Pie Jesu' from Faure's 'Requiem'. I read this poem by Hafiz, a Sufi poet, that was given to Anne and me by our friend, Fr Donal Dorr, when we were going through some hard times.

My Sweet, Crushed Angel
You have not danced so badly, my dear,
Trying to hold hands with the Beautiful One.

You have waltzed with great style,
My sweet, crushed angel,
To have ever neared God's Heart at all.

Our Partner is notoriously difficult to follow,
And even His best musicians are not always easy to hear.
So what if the music has stopped for a while.

So what If the price of admission to the Divine
Is out of reach tonight.

So what, my dear,
If you do not have the ante to gamble for Real Love.

The mind and the body are famous
For holding the heart ransom,
But Hafiz knows the Beloved's eternal habits.
Have patience,

For He will not be able to resist your longing
For long.

You have not danced so badly, my dear,
Trying to kiss the Beautiful One.
You have actually waltzed with tremendous style,
O my sweet,
O my sweet, crushed angel.

from 'I heard God Laughing' renderings
of Hafiz by Daniel Ladinsky

Taking Anne's ashes to the Grail Center near Cape Town

The director of Training for Transformation, Ntombi Nyathi, and teammate, Ginoca Neto Dunstan, met me at Cape Town airport where we collapsed into each other's arms, weeping. There were no words. Back at the Grail Center, both Ntombi and Ginoca visited with me each morning and evening. Their support and caring was lovely. I arranged for a small group of Grail members and friends to plan Anne's funeral mass, with Anne's spiritual advisor, Fr Roger Hickley, presiding. This mass was held in the Sacred Forest where Anne had spent so much time clearing paths, pruning and meditating.

I stood by the entrance to the Sacred Forest to greet friends and relatives. More than 150 people attended with people sitting outside, some in shade and some in the sun. The mass was lovely with Grail members and Anne's two godchildren burying her ashes under a yellowwood tree. After a light lunch, we had a celebration of her life. A few participants from the Training for Transformation program had arranged a series of pictures of Anne from her many years of work and Presence to so many. These displays encircled the entire meeting room. As a training program was in progress at this time, those members from eleven countries, came into the room, one country at a time with a folded flag of their country while we sang, 'Hamba gashle'. They put their flag on the table where a large picture of Anne was mounted. The moderator then opened up time for anyone to say a remembrance of Anne. Some friends from Europe, like Enda Byrne, had come and we were able to meet and share so many memories.

In the afternoon, the family took some of Anne's ashes to the ocean, where she had enjoyed many swims and time to be silent watching the wonderful sea breakers. A week later, with a different nephew, I took her remaining ashes to Knysna, about a five-hour drive east of Cape Town, to be laid to rest with her mother and brother.

I spent another month at the Grail Center, having lunches with the participants, giving a talk once in a while to them, and just spending time with the staff. I also varnished windows and read. I went to Cape Town to visit friends while still trying to take in the absence of Anne by my side.

Life without Anne

Having this need to be 'productive', I began jumping into things where I thought my skills and experience might be helpful. There was also the need to be 'busy' and not get into a lonely space. I continued with activities at Pilgrim Place, including singing in the choir which was, and is, a lovely experience. I continued on committees there, worked with Sally Simmel to restore furniture, gave one session at a course at a college in our town, went to concerts and movies. As Anne's friend, Donna Ambrogi's husband had died three months before Anne, we became very good friends and had similar interests. She kept me going often and we went to the ocean staying in a lovely home up the mountainside of Long Beach to just relax. I also took on the task of holding financial Power of Attorney for three Grail members, as their abilities were diminishing. The United States Grail was looking for national council members so I said yes and was elected.

In 2017, besides going to three National Grail Council meetings, I facilitated five weekend regional workshops in Louisiana, New York City, Cornwall-on-Hudson in the state of New York, Cincinnati, and California here at Pilgrim Place. The aim was to enable Grail members to reflect on our issues, but also to think about the future. This worked quite well in one regional workshop, while in the others, the differences over owning land were lingering. It was worth the try. I found the national Council meetings did not give me energy, as I was used to a more participatory process in looking at the long-term future in organizations, finances, or the issue at hand. In that same year, I took on being on the Grail National Assembly planning meeting with a very dynamic team. We put in place many participatory processes, yet the energy to carry ideas forward to solid programs was moderate. I have not, at the time of writing, found where I can best use my skills and experiences. I was invited to an International Grail meeting to help with the planning of the 100th Anniversary of the Grail with this international group. It was lovely to meet old friends from so many different countries where I had lived.

At this time, US national politics, with Trump at the helm, were getting worse and worse. Over this year I read a number of books and articles on fascism. I gave a program on what Trump was doing to our government agencies; by this time he had made cuts of billions of dollars to more than sixty-six agencies: human rights, environment, poverty programs, housing, and the list goes on. I continue to have deep concerns and fears for us in the USA and globally.

In 2018 and 2019 I went back to the Grail Center in Kleinmond. Each time my visits with friends, staff and participants in programs were enriching. In 2019, the Training for Transformation staff, in light of a major evaluation conducted by one of the biggest funders of this program, suggested that the one-year program be made shorter and held in various regions like Asia/Pacific, eastern, western, southern Africa, Europe, and maybe Latin America. A Think Well was set up with past participants and some of us old timers for six days. By chance, some of us old timers were sitting together at supper when the massacre happened in a mosque in Christchurch, NZ. Around the table were a Muslim from Cape Town, a Jesuit priest from India, a Catholic sociologist from Zimbabwe, a non-professing but deeply spiritual person from Canada and South Africa, and me. We stopped eating and offered a long silent prayer. Then we started talking and for some reason, we found ourselves growing extremely close. When I showed a picture of this group to a friend, he said, 'That is your tribe'. It rang very true.

During 2017-18, an old friend of Anne's, Stephanie Kilroe, had taken on writing Anne's biography. I had sent her all of Anne's 'morning pages'. These were like a journal of Anne's inner work. I did not read them before I sent them to Stephanie as it felt too painful. Stephanie's book was published, by Darton, Longman and Todd in London after the publisher read it in one sitting and said yes. I called them to see if they could get 50 copies of the book to us before the end of March so we could have an informal book launch. The books arrived at Anne's niece's house in Cape Town where I was staying at the end of my trip, and more than 50 people showed up for the launch. It was another moment of remembering the joy and delight Anne brought to us all.

Aging and diminishment

Back at Pilgrim Place in 2019, I held a book launch with several old friends of Anne speaking to the book. I also found that I was needing to stop a few times while walking to our noon meal. Sometimes, I had shortness of breath even while sitting quietly. I saw a heart specialist and had a heart test. On July 30, 2019, the shortness of breath got into 'panting' and I felt like I was drowning – without being in water. I called our 24-hour clinic at Pilgrim Place and the nurse arrived in a few minutes. She insisted we call 911 and an ambulance arrived in less than 5 minutes. We got to the Emergency Room at the hospital – and I had a group of first responders working on me, but I only remember their faces close to mine. I slept, I guess, and was taken to another room.

I was then taken to the operating room and had an angioplasty and a stent put into the main artery in my heart. I was then sent to a recuperating room reserved for those who had had heart surgery. That same night, on Tuesday at about 8 p.m., I went into another similar episode. So, they took me to the Intensive Care Unit.

From what I understand, I had both congenital heart failure and lungs filled with liquid. During the 2 days I was in the ICU, I had extensive work done on my lungs and tests for my heart. They found that I only have 20 per cent strength in my heart and at my age, it should be 35+ per cent. I have been going to cardiac physio-therapy to strengthen my heart since then. While at our noon meal one day, I spoke with a woman whose mother is 95 years old and still lives by herself, cooks, shops, cleans her own house and her heart strength is at 10%. This really lifted a weight off my shoulders. My cardiologist believed I need a pacemaker to keep my heart going, and hopefully strengthens it. Dealing with six medical doctors and the health system is a huge challenge that many of us who are in the United States know about.

I wrote to many friends around the world to tell them of my heart attacks. My psychotherapist in Cape Town wrote back and we had a few sessions on Skype. She said, 'Sally, you allowed Anne to take half your heart. You need to reclaim it and write your own biography.' Our call was in early August 2019. This rang a loud bell and the next day I started writing.

On February 24, 2020 I went into the hospital for the implant of my pacemaker/defibrillator. The surgeon spent 4 hours for a one-hour procedure because of my scarred heart. This caused my heart to be traumatized and fluid gathered around it. I was therefore in the hospital for five days (instead of one day) but the medication drained the fluid and I was able to come home. A dear friend at Pilgrim Place stayed with me for three nights, so I felt emotionally secure. Then of course, the coronavirus hit the country and as I am slightly at risk, I have my main meal delivered to my house, and other friends shop for me for breakfasts and supper food supplies.

Besides taking better care of my health, finding my way around the health care system, and continuing with projects with the Grail and here at Pilgrim Place, I am very focused on the limited actions I can take in relation to the United States national elections in November 2020. As I wrote earlier, this move towards fascism globally, and at a rapid pace in the United States, is frightening.

I am very aware I have not written explicitly about my own spirituality. I do not speak about my faith much, nor am I drawn to lectures about spirituality or faith or theology. Being productive, doing rather than 'being', has been interlaced throughout my life. For me this comes from the New Testament saying, 'I know your works, your toil and your patient endurance, and how you cannot bear with those who are evil, but have tested those who call themselves apostles and are not, and found them to be false. I know you are enduring patiently and bearing up for my name's sake, and you have not grown weary.'

We live in hope. An older Grail member here said recently, then when there is chaos and darkness, there are glimmers of light that come through the cracks. Make those cracks larger, however you can. That is our task and most likely has been our task over the millennium.

In closing

What *best* describes my vocation and Anne's and my vocations? I use Anne's own words from her autobiography as she reflects on our vocation from *A Track to the Water's Edge* by Olive Shreiner.

> This story tells of a young woman searching for the land of freedom, who meets an old wise woman on the banks of a deep and dangerous river. The old woman, Reason, advises her that to get to the land of freedom, she must go down the banks of labor, through the waters of suffering, setting aside her 'cloak of ancient received opinions' and the 'shoes of dependence' on her feet. The young woman asks if many have crossed before, and is told that many have tried. She is reminded of the locusts, some of which tried to cross and were heard of no more. 'Heard of no more?' the young woman exclaims horrified. 'Heard of no more,' Reason repeats, 'but what of that? With their bodies they have built a bridge over which many more could pass. They made a track to the water's edge!' Anne continues: 'We have chosen this theme because we do hope that, with our books we have published and all the work we have done, and on the work of many others, some of whom "are heard of no more", we have helped to make 'a track to the water's edge', contributing to the building of a bridge, which can be used for those who are truly seeking the 'land of freedom'.

Appendix: Letting go as a founder

As the co-author of *Training for Transformation*, Vol. 1-4 and *Training for Transformation In Practice*, I was also the Legislative Director at Church Women United (like a women's branch of the National Council of Churches) in the USA for eight years; co-founded this work in Kenya for seven years and started seven non-profit organizations in South Africa between 1995-2014. The following are some learnings from my mistakes and successes.

Start the work as if you will not be in place for long. As the ancient Chinese guru said, '... and the people will say of the best leaders, we did this ourselves'. When starting a new organization, very early on in the work find a strong team to work with. From this team can emerge a person with a broad vision and the capacity to work well with the team. Leaders emerge, those who keep their eyes on the goal and who encourage a broad range of views, and are not only focused on 'their way to do something'. If one tries to 'own' the work, it can push people away. The 'work' must be 'our work'.

Have another 'passion'. When I was the Legislative Director at Church Women United (CWU) in Washington DC, after eight years there the issue of health care reform became one of the biggest issues in the United States. The CWU national council decided to make health care reform its national priority for three years. I saw we could run workshops using the Freire methods on ethical choices on health care reform. We would target key states in this work and train at least 200+ members to hold workshops in their local congregations and other organizations. The CWU national director then suggested that my assistant in Washington DC become the legislative director so I could head the health care reform initiative workshops in nine key states in the USA. Training animators was my passion and tapped into my strengths. I followed my passion and it felt wonderful to hand over my previous position.

Build a strong team. Building a strong team can be tricky as there are many factors to consider. Often it is possible because there are people with a wide range of skills sets. At other times, one might choose team members because of one factor over another. This was true for me in one project, a local one in a small town, so I thought that all staff should be from this town even if they didn't have experience in the particular field of the project. Some expected enough funds to implement big plans, others were used to working alone, and some were focused on quite narrow outcomes. Of course, tensions grew in the team. I became more 'stubborn' and therefore demanding. New people joined the team and were not always as strongly committed to this local community. Not a good mix for building a team.

Affirmation and feedback sessions. Building a strong team often depends on regular feedback sessions. This can involve authentically saying what you appreciate in each other, and what could be areas of improvement. Affirmation builds confidence in oneself and the ability to take on more responsibilities. It also builds a stronger team. When giving feedback on where a person needs to improve, if it is more personal that feedback should be on a one-to-one basis rather than in the whole group. In the whole group questions like 'where do you need help or support to meet your goals on time?' or 'where do you think you need to improve and build' (on what the person says about themselves). Keep affirming good work and affirming the team. Sometimes laugh at yourself; we all have blind spots and areas where we ourselves can improve. Graciously accept negative feedback from others.

Becoming self-reliant. When selecting members for a strong team, serious conversations must be held before employment on the issue of who has what authority. Usually the founder, as part of the team, will have the most authority at the beginning. This lessens as the team takes up more responsibilities and delivers outcomes in their particular area of work. As the team grows into its work and produces outcomes related to the goals, new leaders will emerge. Some will even start to help to fundraise. Often a dilemma of authority can block the way to teams becoming self-reliant.

Patience. Sometimes one team member has a deep passion for the project. Honoring their input is important but can take an organization in a direction that is hard to sustain. If one takes on such a new project without capable staff to do the work, this can entail years to build up a strong team and a possible new director. It requires loads of patience to build a strong team for the long haul. It also means not 'letting go' too fast in handing over the leadership, which is difficult if this is not your main passion.

Push potential leaders 'over a cliff' and they will fly. At the point of handing over an organization, it can mean truly letting go. As one new director said to me months later, I just pushed her over the cliff, and then she realized she could fly. Obviously, all of the funders and income sources were soundly in place with the new directors, who have since started to build their own relationships with the funders.

Recognize burnout in oneself. Being self-aware, of our own behavior and attitudes, is important as a founder or director of an organization. If one finds oneself becoming more irritated, short-tempered or not feeling fully engaged with, or with less energy for, this 'work', this can drag down the whole organization. Find another passion. Speak to some close friends to get some feedback and discuss a possible timeline of turning over the organization to others. This could be one of the indicators that it is time to 'let go'.